2, 3 JOHN & JUDE

Truth and Danger in the Church

Richard Caldwell

ISBN: 978-1-934952-43-6

DEDICATION

To Founders Baptist Church. Words cannot express my love and appreciation for you.

CONTENTS

ACKNOWLEDGMENTS

I am once again grateful to Jim and Gail Swindle for their editorial insight and painstaking labors in bringing another volume in this series to fruition. I also want to thank Jeremy Loftin, Juan Carlos Claveria, and Larry Lartigue for their partnership in this ministry of the Word.

1
TRUTH AND LOVE
(2 John 1-3)

The little book of 2 John has a big message, a very important message for today. It is a call for discernment in the matters of **truth**, **love** and **hospitality**, which is just one specific application of truth and love. Discernment is the application of truth and love in an individual life. We learn to base our decisions on, limit our choices to, yield in our attitudes to, that which pleases God. So, **in truth** this is a book about truth, and love, and living.

Though the New Testament letters often bear the same basic format as other letters of their time, they are very different in their substance. Often the greeting is pregnant with a theme or a concern that will be unfolded throughout the rest of the letter, as is the case in this one.

Internal indicators and external testimony both lead us to conclude that it was the apostle John who penned this letter, probably from Ephesus. He is dealing with many of the same concerns that we find in the book of 1 John. However, from the beginning of this letter, it is clear they are more personal and specific in relating to truth and love. He does not want these believers left in spiritual danger through misunderstanding these things.

The aged apostle is instructing the readers about a very dangerous deception. There are many false Christs at work in their world. They have gone astray, misunderstanding the incarnation and misunderstanding God and His Son.

They are demonstrating and propagating a false gospel. John wants his readers to hold fast to the truth and to know and express the love that exists in the truth. That means giving no assistance to those who would propagate any message contrary to the truth and the love that are found in the true God and His Son.

John writes toward the end of the 1st century, a time when the church is dealing with the beginnings of what will eventually turn into the heretical movement known as Gnosticism. He is concerned, because some believers are not only exposing themselves to the errors of the false teachers, but are misunderstanding the requirement of Christian hospitality and what it means to really love people. As a result, they are giving aid to those who preach things that are false and very dangerous.

THE AUTHOR AND THE RECIPIENTS OF THE LETTER (:1a)

The elder

The apostle John is the author, but he does not refer to himself by name nor by the title of apostle. He calls himself *the elder.* Apparently, his readers know him well and love him. They are not in doubt about his apostleship. The term *elder* is used in more than one way in the New Testament. It can refer simply to age. John, by this time, is certainly an old man. *Elder* can be used in a formal way to refer to the office of leadership found in one particular local church. John's role is larger than that, though he would serve in that way for any local church where he serves. In this case, it is probably the church at Ephesus. *Elder* can also be used, as it is here, to speak of an apostle, one of those who are the respected messengers of the gospel from the very beginning. On John's part, it is an affectionate way to address these people while warmly pointing to his authority. What he's writing is both loving and important. They must hear him. My friend Danny Akin wrote of this verse:

> The fact that the apostle John was by now an old man and that he also held a special position and authority as the last surviving apostle makes this title especially fitting. He had no need to assert his apostleship. That was common knowledge and he could appeal

to them in a more tender fashion. His standing with those to whom he was writing was well established.[1]

John's reference to himself as *the elder* is a good reminder that discernment in the Christian is not instant. It must grow as we mature. Yet even time and Bible knowledge alone do not explain discernment. Age, time, experience, knowledge, practice, and obedience in the way of truth and love, yield greater and greater discernment. Increasingly, it is not only the Christian who has the truth, it is the truth that has the Christian.

Stephen Charnock wrote, "A man may be theologically knowing and spiritually ignorant."[2] But we don't always have those two stark extremes. You can be theologically knowing and not spiritually ignorant, yet not as spiritually mature as you will become.

We are living in a time of youthful foolishness and overconfidence, including in the church and in the ministry. There are practical novices who imagine they have arrived because they know some things, have some training, or possess some giftedness. They often gather with other novices, convincing one another that they aren't novices and labeling the older ones in the faith as foolish. If this is you, be warned that it is a very, very unwise course. It really reveals your own immaturity. Those who are most mature in the faith will have the greatest respect for those who are older in the faith. Humility is the dress of maturity and discernment. In one sense, the discernment of these people to whom John is writing will be immediately tested by seeing if they will listen to *the elder*.

No one would venture to undertake the building of a house were he not an architect, nor will anyone attempt the cure of sick bodies who is not a skilled physician; but even though many urge him, will beg off, and will not be ashamed to own his ignorance; and shall

---

[1] Daniel L. Akin, *1, 2, 3 John*, vol. 38, The New American Commentary (Nashville: Broadman & Holman Publishers, 2001), 219.

[2] Elliot Ritzema, ed., *300 Quotations for Preachers* (Bellingham, WA: Lexham Press, 2012).

he who is going to have the care of so many souls entrusted to him, not examine himself beforehand? —John Chrysostom[3]

The elect lady

People have long debated the identity of the elect lady and her children. There are two main views. Some say we should read this in a natural and straightforward fashion and see this as a particular woman and her children. Later, John would be referring to her sister and to her nephews and nieces. That is certainly a possibility, but I am among those who believe John is speaking of a church and a sister church. The children would be individual members of those churches. John referred to the church in family terms once before, in 1 Jn 2:13-14. There, he spoke of fathers, young men, and children. Also, what he writes here in his second letter reads equally as well if we understand this as an example of metaphorical language, a church, instead of an individual. This is a familiar technique. We know what people mean when they refer to a ship using a feminine pronoun. "She sailed well today," a ship's captain may say.

The letter's meaning and application remain the same, whether the elect lady is an individual or a church. The truth must be lived out on an individual basis. John's letter calls for individual choice.

The lady is elect.

This church is an elect group of people, or this woman is an elect individual. Either way, the truth is emphasized that a believer's salvation is explained by the *sovereign choice of God.*

God emphasizes His sovereignty in salvation.

Everything John says in this letter dealing with the Christian demonstrates that God chose these people for salvation before time. God's Word reminds us of this regularly. It's good for us to reflect often on God's choice of us and of others.

---

[3] Ibid.

THE NATURE OF THEIR RELATIONSHIP TO EACH OTHER AND ITS CAUSE (:1b-2)

God's choice—both of her and of others—results in a unique relationship that John describes as her and her children.

John loves her and her children in the truth (:1b)

He means either that he loves them in their common relationship to the truth, or that he loves them in the sphere or context of the truth of the gospel, the truth of Christ. Both are true.

Everyone who knows the truth loves her and her children (:1c)

Not only John, but every Christian loves them. All who know the truth will love the people of God.

The reason for this love: The truth that abides in God's people and will be with God's people forever (:1d)

Truth and love are never enemies—they are always together.

Many people think truth and love oppose each other, but they are never enemies. Love is in the truth, and wherever truth has made its entrance, love is the result. It's hard to know where truth begins and love ends, or where love begins and truth ends. Where one is, the other is. There is no real love apart from the presence of God's truth, and there is no real presence of God's truth without the product of love. True truth and true love are in absolute agreement. They need no reconciliation, because they aren't enemies. This agreement is universally found wherever truth and love exist.

Those who want to pit love against the truth have a perverted view of love. They want us to "love" them by affirming them. Some will argue that they want us to love them while they pursue a particular sinful path. Others will insist that their sin really isn't sin, and will insist that we celebrate it. If we won't celebrate it, they call us bigots. Those in the church who are not quite so brazen may go along with such reasoning, excusing their affirmation of sin by the thought that they are loving the person.

5

The objects of this love are those chosen by God.

The objects of this love are those who are chosen by God—here, the elect lady and her children, whether she's an individual or a church. Everyone who knows the truth loves those chosen by God for salvation.

The truth he has in mind exists now in God's people and abides with them forever.

The people being described are now in the truth, the truth is now in them, and it will remain with them forever. In the lives of believers, we find both the internal operation of truth and the objective possession of truth. They have embraced the truth, and by God's grace, they'll never let it go. What a powerful description of the truth and love that exist in salvation, and how those who have it set this love on each other!

THE NATURE OF THEIR RELATIONSHIP TO GOD AND ITS ASSURANCES (:3)

Wherever this truth and love exist, an assurance also exists.

What we have: Grace, mercy and peace.

We can know, and need to know, that we go forward in life and to eternity with the *grace* of God, the multiplied *mercies* of God, and the *peace* of God. We know God's grace, mercy and peace, in all their multiple forms. Name any aspect of what grace is, or any aspect of what mercy is, or any aspect of what peace is, and Scripture will demonstrate that it is the possession of the Christian. These things have been ours and will be ours in the days to come. This is holy confidence and holy rest.

We know **grace** in terms of: (1) all of God's undeserved favor, (2) a standing of complete acceptance in Christ, apart from our works, and (3) God's powerful and undeserved work in us and through us.

We know **mercy** in all its multiple forms: in forgiveness, joys, pleasures, and patience. Not only do we know God giving us things we don't deserve, but we know God sparing us from things that we do deserve.

We know **peace** in all its multiple forms: peace with God and the peace that comes from God. It is felt in our relationships with others and in our own souls, regardless of circumstances.

6

Who gave us what we have

We have these assurances because these things come to us from God the Father and from the Son of the Father, Jesus Christ. This is crucial in view of the heresies John is battling, sort of a seed form of what will eventually grow into Gnosticism. The error deals with the incarnation, who Jesus is, and, therefore, with who God is. In this verse, we see the Father and Jesus presented as distinct in person but one in divine nature. What we have received from the Father, we have received from the Son, and yet they can be distinguished in terms of their persons.

The preposition παϱά (*para*, from) is used twice, once for the Father and once for the Son, emphasizing equality in terms of the source of these blessings. You cannot dishonor Jesus and honor the Father. You need to understand who Jesus is. He's God in human flesh, the second person of the Trinity.

Where we receive what we have

With this final reference to truth and love, as well as <u>all</u> the references to truth and love, we have come to know the truth <u>in God, by God's Son, Jesus</u>. It is the truth of the gospel, not merely grasped on an intellectual level but also experienced in salvation.

Eph 4:17 *Now this I say and testify in the Lord, that you must no longer walk as the Gentiles do, in the futility of their minds. 18 They are darkened in their understanding, alienated from the life of God because of the ignorance that is in them, due to their hardness of heart. 19 They have become callous and have given themselves up to sensuality, greedy to practice every kind of impurity. 20 But that is not the way you learned Christ!-- 21 assuming that you have heard about him and were taught in him, as the truth is in Jesus*

A final word on the connection between truth, love, and practical obedience

John Newton expressed it well:

Assurance grows by repeated conflict, by our repeated experimental proof of the Lord's power and goodness to save; when we have been brought very low and helped, sorely wounded and healed, cast down and raised again, have given up all hope, and been suddenly snatched from danger, and placed in safety; and when these things have been repeated to us and in us a thousand times over, we begin to learn to trust simply to the word and power of God, beyond and against appearances: and this trust, when habitual and strong, bears the name of assurance; for even assurance has degrees.[4]

---

[4] Ibid.

2
THE JOY OF GODLY PEOPLE
(2 John 4-6)

As we have seen, the book of 2 John is a call for discernment in the matters of **truth**, love and hospitality, which is just one specific application of truth and love. It is a book about truth, and love, and living. At the same time, it also gives us insight into what motivates godly pastoral leadership. The aged apostle John is shepherding these people. He is concerned about their spiritual condition and about their spiritual choices. This letter reveals his heart as a shepherd. It reveals what concerns him and what would comfort him.

The body of the letter is divided into two issues. John addresses the standard for life within the family of God (:4-6), and spiritual dangers that exist outside the family of God (:7-11). These are still concerns for every faithful pastor and for every godly person who cares for those who profess Christ. These areas matter to us if we're striving to be godly parents, godly friends, and wherever we find ourselves responsible for another person in the context of ministry. Our interest is in their relationship to the church and to the world— to that which threatens the church. In this chapter, the focus will be on their relationship to the church.

In verses 4-6, John focuses on how the children of God are relating to each other. We see a godly man's rejoicing (:4), a godly man's request (:5), and a godly man's reminder (:6). If you are doing well spiritually, then your relationship to the church will be godly and healthy, which means it will be

9

2 JOHN 4-6

biblically obedient. Never imagine or pretend that you are doing well spiritually when your relationship to the Lord's people in the local church is not healthy.

A GODLY MAN'S REJOICING (:4)

John begins with what gives his heart joy. We'd do well to examine our joy in comparison with his. Do we share his joy when we think about the lives of others?

The reality of his joy

The word for joy in the text is followed by an adverb (λίαν, lian) that means "exceedingly" or "very much." John's heart is filled with (passive verb) great joy over what he is about to describe. It is a sincere and intense joy.

Whatever brings joy to our hearts is a commentary on our spiritual condition, our spiritual concerns and our spiritual maturity. Parenting is an example of how we change as our joys change. Have you found that your reasons for rejoicing change as the Lord changes your life? Have you found that your reasons for rejoicing change as you get older in the faith and mature as a Christian? Perhaps in your younger years, your greatest joys were found in the accomplishments of your children, accomplishments that really have very little to do with Christ or with their character. You may have rejoiced in their natural gifts or in their temporal accomplishments. But as you have grown in Christ, you have an increasing understanding of the brevity of life and the seriousness of eternity. You are far less focused on natural gifts and temporal achievements and far more focused on the soul. You have changed, and your perspective has changed.

The same can be said in the context of ministry. Pastors grow, too. Many younger men in the ministry know what they should rejoice in. They know the biblical—and therefore correct—priorities and reasons for rejoicing. However, they may find that it is a battle to get their heart to agree with their head. They want to be successful and to achieve on behalf of the kingdom. It is not that their motives are entirely impure, but their perspectives still reflect their youthfulness, and the years of maturity still lie ahead. As they grow, buildings and budgets and statistics mean far less to them than the condition of their people. The reason for John's joy is a mature one.

The reason for his joy

John's heart is full of joy because he has learned (whether personally or by report) that some of the children of this lady are *walking in the truth*. By *some*, he does not mean that some are, and some aren't. He means that at least some are. He sees these people whom he has met with as representative of the church, or he is merely commenting on his knowledge of these people, without any reference to the others. Regardless, he says that this knowledge has given him cause for great rejoicing, which is not an isolated instance on his part. This is the kind of news he lives for.

3 John 1:1 *The elder to the beloved Gaius, whom I love in truth. ² Beloved, I pray that all may go well with you and that you may be in good health, as it goes well with your soul. ³ For I rejoiced greatly when the brothers came and testified to your truth, as indeed you are walking in the truth. ⁴ I have no greater joy than to hear that my children are walking in the truth.*

WALKING IN THE TRUTH

The truth

The truth is the truth of Christ and the truth of the gospel—all the truth that belongs to that realm. We know this is what he means by way of contrast. He talks about what concerns him in :7-11. He is concerned about anything that doesn't agree with this truth—the truth of who Jesus is, and the teaching that accords with that truth. Everything contrary to it is deadly for the individual who receives it, and deadly for all whom they influence.

The walk

To walk in that truth is to live in agreement with it—in our thinking, our teaching, our living, and our loving. What is true of John, in this case, is true of any godly person. A godly person rejoices when they see the truth of God's Son and God's word taking real root in a person's life. We rejoice when we see people…

- Making choices that say that Jesus has first place in their lives
- Making choices that say that they are submissive to Scripture
- Reorganizing their priorities to honor God, love His church, and obey Scripture
- Learning the truth, believing, living and proclaiming it
- Sacrificing on behalf of ministry

All these things, and others, speak of Scripture taking root in a person's life, which speaks of Christ being preeminent in their lives. Seeing these things brings great joy to the hearts of the godly. This rejoicing speaks of real fellowship with the Father, and it demonstrates real submission to the Father. Believers are commanded to live like this. The result is a life with joys that match John's, walking in ways that bring joy to the heart of a godly man, and knowing joy when we look at the lives of others who are walking in truth.

A GODLY MAN'S REQUEST (:5)

In light of this joy, John requests that we (believers) love one another. This is obedience within the family of God, a life that walks in the truth of Christ. It is the life of mutual love—believers loving one another.

An authoritative request

This is a gentle and warm way of communicating what is, in fact, a command. We know it's a command because he reminds them that this is *not ... a new commandment,* but one they *had from the beginning.*

An established request

False teachers offer something new (and false), while the true teacher applies what is true from the beginning. In John we have a great example of what shepherding people involves. It is not giving them something new but reminding them of what has already been revealed in Jesus Christ. By the way, you aren't doing well when you can't hear long-established truths with fresh ears. We need to receive established truths with great joy in our hearts.

A profound and practical request

In the church, we should be exhorting one another regularly to **live** the love of God. Many of the issues we deal with in the life of the local church could be addressed with this simple command, *Love one another.*

- When people are at odds with each other in the church—Love each other!
- When something needs to be done that will require time and sacrifice—Love God's people.
- When our zeal for the most basic things in the Christian life seems to be waning—church attendance, fellowship, discipleship, service—Love God and your brethren.

- When sin has been committed and confession is needed, or forgiveness is needed—Love each other.
- When a need arises in the life of someone and we have the means to meet that need—Love one another.
- When difficulties arise in a marriage or between children in a home—Love each other.

We **must** love one another. God commands it. This is a specific kind of love, God's love. It requires a submissive response to His truth in all areas of life. We are commanded to deal with others according to His standards of divine love.

A GODLY MAN'S REMINDER (:6)

We are reminded yet again that genuinely embracing the truth and genuinely expressing of the love of God are inseparable. If you're really walking in the truth, you're walking in love. Conversely, if you're really walking in love, it's according to the truth. Don't empty obedience of its loving heart, and don't sentimentalize what love is, emptying it of all standards. Walking in love is according to the truth. This is what God has commanded, and all His commandments can be summed up in these words.

Matthew 22:36 *"Teacher, which is the great commandment in the Law?"* *37 And he said to him, "You shall love the Lord your God with all your heart and with all your soul and with all your mind. 38 This is the great and first commandment. 39 And a second is like it: You shall love your neighbor as yourself. 40 On these two commandments depend all the Law and the Prophets."*

Galatians 5:13 *For you were called to freedom, brothers. Only do not use your freedom as an opportunity for the flesh, but through love serve one another. 14 For the whole law is fulfilled in one word: "You shall love your neighbor as yourself."*

The details of God's commandments do matter, but we need to live them out in the context of loving God and loving people. Living out that commandment is a powerful apologetic. It speaks of the reality of a relationship to Jesus.

John 13:35 *By this all people will know that you are my disciples, if you have love for one another.*

"The early Latin writer, Tertullian of Carthage, declared that the one thing that converted him to Christianity was not the arguments they gave him, because he could find a counterpoint for every argument they would present. 'But they demonstrated something I didn't have. The thing that converted me to Christianity was the way they loved each other.'"[5]

Godly people walk in truth and love. They rejoice greatly whenever they meet with people who are walking in truth and love. Truth and love should never be separated.

---

[5] G. Curtis Jones, *1000 Illustrations for Preaching and Teaching* (Nashville, TN: Broadman & Holman Publishers, 1986), 220.

3
TRUTH, LOVE, AND DECEIVERS
(2 John 7)

One of the great issues that faces every new generation of believers is how to respond to the spiritual dangers that arise against the church. The New Testament is clear that we will deal with dangers from within the church, as well as those that seek to make inroads into the church from outside it. Every new generation must learn, embrace, and live out the way which God has revealed. We need to believe God, convinced that His way of dealing with these things is the only way to deal with them. This is a constant concern for the apostles in the early church.

Acts 20:29 *I know that after my departure fierce wolves will come in among you, not sparing the flock; ³⁰ and from among your own selves will arise men speaking twisted things, to draw away the disciples after them. ³¹ Therefore be alert, remembering that for three years I did not cease night or day to admonish every one with tears.*

As you can hear in Paul's words, this is no small issue, but something that he's been warning about constantly. It has moved him to tears, because the souls of people are at stake. The future of the church is at stake. It is also clear that these dangers are in the form of men who will **teach things** contrary to the truth. The first and foremost danger is doctrinal.

When people are skeptical of spiritual leaders, their skepticism often centers on the **behavior** of those in leadership. It is true that false teachers are often described in the New Testament in terms of their immorality or their greed, but this is the **fruit** that accompanies those that live sinful lifestyles. The real threat is the **teaching** associated with demons, propagated by these ungodly men. They **have embraced and disseminated error**. The result is that people are drawn away from the truth. In the above passage from Acts 20, Paul describes them as men *speaking twisted things*. The corruption that comes from their mouths is then accompanied by the corruption that shows up in their lives. This is the battle—apostolic doctrine versus demonic doctrine, truth versus lies.

2 Peter 2:1 *But false prophets also arose among the people, just as there will be false teachers among you, who will secretly bring in destructive heresies, even denying the Master who bought them, bringing upon themselves swift destruction.*

Jude 1:3 *Beloved, although I was very eager to write to you about our common salvation, I found it necessary to write appealing to you to contend for the faith that was once for all delivered to the saints. ⁴ For certain people have crept in unnoticed who long ago were designated for this condemnation, ungodly people, who pervert the grace of our God into sensuality and deny our only Master and Lord, Jesus Christ.*

1 Tim 4:1 *Now the Spirit expressly says that in later times some will depart from the faith by devoting themselves to deceitful spirits and teachings of demons, ² through the insincerity of liars whose consciences are seared, ³ who forbid marriage and require abstinence from foods that God created to be received with thanksgiving by those who believe and know the truth.*

This is a letter about truth and love and the discernment which flows from them. From this passage we can draw four principles about how truth and love confront false teachers and false teaching.

A COMMITMENT TO TRUTH AND LOVE PREPARES THE CHURCH TO WITHSTAND FALSE TEACHERS (:7a)

Verse 7 begins with the little connective conjunction Ότι (Hoti), translated *for* or *because*. We must walk in love and truth, because many false teachers *have gone out into the world*. The command to walk in the truth is vital for the church, not only because of what is required of us in the family of God, but also in view of what is happening in the world. We must obey God by walking in truth and love. This is essential—not only so that we might please Him inside the church, but also as we face the dangers that threaten the church. **Keep the truth, and the truth will keep you. Walk in the truth, and the truth protects you.** This functions in two ways.

Truth and love define the community.

A commitment to truth and love as the Bible reveals them enables us to know where the community actually exists. Where you find the Lord's church, you find the truth and the love of God. One of the great battles for modern evangelicalism is identifying what the church is. It's not a place. It's a people.

Marvin Olasky interviewed Al Mohler for *World* Magazine. Note Mohler's response to the following question:

> Olasky: What is your greatest concern for the local church these days?
>
> Mohler: Martin Luther famously said the church is where the Word of God is rightly preached and ordinances rightly administered. Then he said it all starts with the first mark of the church, where the Word of God is rightly preached. That is the one thing that must happen, and my greatest fear is that that is the one thing that won't happen. If you have a Reformation model of the church, which we hope is the New Testament model of the church, then as Paul said to Timothy, whatever you do in season and out of season, one thing you have to do is to preach the Word, and let the Word do its work. Luther explained the Reformation in Wittenberg by saying, I preached and then I went to sleep—and while I slept the Lord did this thing. You have to trust the Lord will do this thing.

The church is composed of those people who have believed the truth and who belong to the truth. It is a walk in truth and light that identifies the Christian. The New Testament describes believers in the following way:

1 John 1:6 *If we say we have fellowship with him while we walk in darkness, we lie and do not practice the truth. ⁷ But if we walk in the light, as he is in the light, we have fellowship with one another, and the blood of Jesus his Son cleanses us from all sin.*

Equally, Christians are identified as those who walk in love.

1 John 4:8 *The one who does not love does not know God, for God is love.*

1 John 4:12 *No one has beheld God at any time; if we love one another, God abides in us, and His love is perfected in us.*

1 John 4:16 *So we have come to know and to believe the love that God has for us. God is love, and whoever abides in love abides in God, and God abides in him.*

Truth and love defend the community.

It is crucial to define who really belongs in the church and who doesn't. When we are committed to truth and love, we must protect the community by rejecting all that doesn't fit with truth and love. To stand against false teaching, you must be able to identify it. It is known both by its substance and its spirit. When we have God's truth and God's love, we are equipped to identify false teaching. This is crucial, because the world is full of dangerous imposters. In John's words, *many deceivers have gone out into the world.* The word is πλάνος (planos) and here means a deceiver, an imposter. There aren't just a few of them. There are multiplied deceivers who have *gone out* into the world. *Gone out* could mean one of two things—or perhaps he had both in mind.

First, he could mean that they have left the place of orthodoxy as seen in 1 John 2:19. Second, he could merely be reminding us that just as genuine believers have a missionary mandate, so Satan has his emissaries disseminating lies. There is a parallel work of world outreach going on.

A CONTINUING CONFESSION OF TRUTH AND LOVE IS THE STANDARD FOR IDENTIFYING FALSE TEACHERS (:7b)

The truth of God in Jesus Christ, and a love that accords with that truth, becomes an informing standard by which discernment is learned and practiced.

First, consider what is **not** the standard. The standard for identifying false teachers is not their manner, age, appearance, friendliness, humor or intelligence. Nor is the standard a selective few portions of what they say, treating it like it's their whole message. Often, there is plenty to be concerned about, but their hearers ignore it. They choose to focus on that which allows them to follow a particular teacher for their listening enjoyment.

We must measure teachers by comparing their beliefs and teachings with Scripture. In this text, the standard for identifying these false teachers is faithfulness to love and truth as embodied in Jesus Himself. Jesus is the truth, and He is love. Jesus is God in human flesh. This Jesus must be believed in and must be loved.

These particular false teachers have been identified by <u>what they will not say</u>. This is very important. False teachers are known not only by what they say but by what they refuse to acknowledge, and what they will not say.

The truth concerning Jesus

A true teacher embraces this never-expiring confession (it's present tense) that Jesus the Christ is come in the flesh, and that He is God incarnate. If you have Jesus wrong, you have everything wrong. If you are wrong about the person and nature of Jesus of Nazareth, then your entire theology is wrong. If your theology is wrong, you cannot possibly understand His work. You are not saved by a faith in just <u>any</u> Jesus. People are saved when they place their faith in the <u>true</u> Jesus, the Jesus of the Bible.

As John writes this letter, a battle is going on with the beginnings of what will one day become a full-blown gnostic heresy. In John's world, there is already Docetism at work. In his world, because of Platonic philosophy, there are people with a dualistic idea saying that what is spirit is good and what is material is evil.[6] They do not believe that God, in the person of the Son, would unite Himself with a human nature, being God and man at the same time.

James P. Boyce, in *Abstract of Systematic Theology*, makes plain the importance of understanding the Trinity if one is to understand Jesus.

> I. The doctrine of the Trinity lies at the foundation of that of Christ's Person. That doctrine is that three persons subsist in one divine nature. It was one of these persons, and not the divine nature itself, that became incarnate.
>
> 1. It was not the Godhead that became incarnate, but one of the persons of the Godhead.

---

[6] Gnosticism includes the idea that people need secret knowledge as the means to salvation. Docetism is the idea that Jesus only seemed to be human; that his sufferings were apparent, but not real, and that he rose with a spiritual, not real, body. Platonism is derived from the ideas of the Greek philosopher Plato.

2. It was not the Father, and the Son, and the Spirit, but it was the Son alone.

3. It was not God abstractly and unitedly, but God personally, the Word that was with God, and that was God, that was made flesh.

4. It was not, therefore, that which was common to the three persons that assumed our nature; but it was that which, in the economy[7] of the Trinity, is distinguished from the others.

5. It was, therefore, not the divine nature or essence, but a person who subsists in that divine nature equally with the others, yet who is distinguished, in his relation to that divine nature, from the other persons of the Trinity.

Boyce continues by saying the following:

> The doctrine of the Trinity is therefore essentially involved in that of the Person of Christ. It is because of the fact of individual personality in the divine Being, by virtue of which, though his nature and essence and being are so one that he is one God, he is yet three-fold, that personal distinctions also exist, and that one person, who is God, can become incarnate without involving the incarnation of the other persons.
>
> Personal distinctions in the Trinity are not necessary to the incarnation of God, but are to that of a divine person.
>
> They are also necessary to the work which Christ performed. Were God only one person, he could not manifest rule, and yet empty himself of it; could not send, and yet be sent; could not be lawgiver, and also voluntary subject; could not make atonement, and yet receive it; could not pour out wrath, and yet endure it.
>
> The Scriptures, therefore, persistently teach, not that "God came," "was sent," "was made flesh," but that God "gave his only-begotten Son," "sent his Son not to condemn the world," "sent forth his Son made of a woman," "sent his only-begotten Son into the world," and that "the Father sent the Son to be the Saviour of the world." Indeed, the first chapter of John, which sets forth the

---

[7] "Economy" here means household administration or management.

doctrines of the Incarnation and Trinity, plainly declares (John 1:18): "No man hath seen God at any time; the only-begotten Son, which is in the bosom of the Father, he hath declared him."[8]

These false teachers have refused to confess the true nature of Jesus Who is fully God and fully Man, the truth that we explain with the word Trinity. They would not affirm that the Son of God came from heaven to earth, took to Himself a real human nature and was and is the Son of God. Today, there are many false teachers who reject the truth about the Father, the Son and the Holy Spirit. Therefore, they are outside the truth and are to be rejected.

Love for the Jesus who is true

False teachers exist outside the love of God. They do not love the true Jesus, nor do they embrace the true gospel. They reject the true God.

1 Corinthians 16:22 *If anyone has no love for the Lord, let him be accursed. Our Lord, come! [23] The grace of the Lord Jesus be with you. [24] My love be with you all in Christ Jesus. Amen.*

A commitment to truth and love prepares the church to withstand the false teachers. The confession of truth and love, as it is in Jesus, enables us to identify the false teachers. Any individual who stands outside the truth and love of Christ is the deceiver and the antichrist. **This figure is not benign but harmful.** There is an endless trail of false religionists in our day, many of whom are made famous by television. Anyone who would pervert the message of Scripture concerning the identity of God, Christ, the Spirit, or the gospel, is dangerous.

God has revealed the way to deal with false teachers and false teaching. He treats this as a serious issue, and so should we. In the next chapter, we'll consider the importance of continuing in truth and love.

---

[8] James Petigru Boyce, *Abstract of Systematic Theology* (Bellingham, WA: Logos Bible Software, 2010), 272-273.

4
TRUTH, LOVE, AND DRAWING THE LINES
(2 John 8-11)

We are learning about how truth, love, and discernment function together. Love exists in the realm of truth, and truth operates in the realm of love. Where truth and love exist, the people of God are learning discernment.

In the last chapter, we saw that a commitment to the truth and love of God is both a preserving force in the life of the church (it prepares the church to withstand false teachers) and the discerning standard for the life of the church (it reveals who are the false teachers).

Truth and love define who is in the community and identify who is a danger to the community.

CONTINUING IN TRUTH AND LOVE IS THE DISTINCTION BETWEEN TRUE BELIEVERS AND FALSE TEACHERS (:8-9)

A command for the community (:8a)

John has a warning for these people—in fact, it is a command. It is imperative to be on the alert, to *watch* themselves, so that they are not drawn away outside the teaching of Christ.

Some manuscripts have *you* in this verse instead of *we*. Both the ESV and NASB reflect the belief that *we* is most likely the original. John is concerned that the false teachers could influence these people in a way that would jeopardize the spiritual work of himself and others, as well as the spiritual work they felt to be true in their own lives. At risk is the good work of gospel ministry.

John's work is the unique work of an apostle. To lose what he had worked for, was to walk away from apostolic doctrine.

John's work is also the work of a shepherd, which is shared by all pastors. True shepherds labor on behalf of the Chief Shepherd in the interest of your spiritual wellbeing. They realize that you are Christ's and that you are also theirs. You represent a divinely given responsibility for which they are to be faithful. You represent their labors, their passions, their prayers, their concerns, and their teaching. You are their work in the Lord.

Paul reveals this same attitude:

1 Corinthians 9:1 *...Are not you my workmanship in the Lord?*

1 Corinthians 4:15 *For though you have countless guides in Christ, you do not have many fathers. For I became your father in Christ Jesus through the gospel. ¹⁶ I urge you, then, be imitators of me. ¹⁷ I sent you Timothy ... to remind you of my ways in Christ, as I teach them everywhere in every church.*

Note the personal nature of this. Paul is writing this, not on behalf of the apostles as a group, but for himself. There are individual roles in the realm of spiritual leadership. This does not mean that Paul views himself as a spiritual lone ranger, but as a coworker in the larger work. His ministry is a personal and passionate responsibility.

Romans 15:20 *...I make it my ambition to preach the gospel, not where Christ has already been named, lest I build on someone else's foundation,*

1 Corinthians 3:6 *I planted, Apollos watered, but God gave the growth. ⁷ So neither he who plants nor he who waters is anything, but only God who gives the growth. ⁸ He who plants and he who waters are one, and each will receive his wages according to his labor. ⁹ For we are God's fellow workers. You are God's field, God's building. ¹⁰ According to the grace of God given to me, like a skilled master builder I laid a foundation, and someone else is building upon it. Let each one take care how he builds upon it. ¹¹ For no one can lay a foundation other than that which is laid, which is Jesus Christ.*

Acts 20:31 *Therefore be alert, remembering that for three years I did not cease night or day to admonish every one with tears.*

See also 1 Thessalonians 2:6-12.

Peter urges all elders to see their work in this way. Shepherding the people of God is a personal investment.

1 Peter 5:2 *shepherd the flock of God that is among you, exercising oversight, not under compulsion, but willingly, as God would have you; not for shameful gain, but eagerly;* *³ not domineering over those in your charge, but being examples to the flock. ⁴ And when the chief Shepherd appears, you will receive the unfading crown of glory.*

John has worked for these people to know Christ, the truth, the true God, and to live lives that honor God. These false teachers are a threat to that work, the exact opposite of what John has been working for.

- Instead of truth, they bring deception.
- Instead of Christ, they bring the spirit of antichrist.
- Instead of eternal life, they bring eternal damnation.

John is passionately and authoritatively alerting them to watch themselves so that they are not drawn away from the things that faithful shepherds have worked so hard to established in them.

This tells us two very important things.

1. False teachers and false doctrine are not to be treated lightly – they represent a <u>real</u> danger to the church, not an imaginary one or simply a theoretical one. You, child of God, are not to entertain what's false but are to take the truth you have been taught and reject <u>anything and everything that doesn't accord with it.</u>
2. The church has a responsibility to be vigilant in this area.

Individual believers and the church as a whole, are to heed what John says here. They are to listen diligently and heed God's faithful words that have already been entrusted to them.

A course for the community (:8b)

The disaster envisioned

The apostle wants them to be vigilant so that their progress in the faith is not lost, in the sense of eternal loss. In this statement, John must certainly include some who would follow in the footsteps of the false teachers who apostatized. He mentions this in the very next verse.

Some don't believe eternal life is in view here, because John speaks of fullness of reward. They take this to mean rewards for service that belong to believers. However, the context makes plain that the loss being considered is the most serious kind possible, everlasting damnation.

My friend, Tom Schreiner, makes the case well.

> The context refers to deceivers and antichrists who have a seriously deficient Christology. John does not think their error is insignificant but damning, according to verse 7. Moreover, verse 9 immediately follows the warning in verse 8, and it shows that eternal life is in view. Those who "progress" and do not continue in orthodox teaching do not have God. Conversely, those who continue in the faith have "both the Father and the Son." Deviation from the teaching here has ultimate consequences, since those who are unfaithful do not even have God. Given that verse 8 is folded between verses 7 and 9 and these verses have to do with whether one belongs to God, the warning in verse 8 should be understood as referring to eternal life.[9]

The desired end

John desires that they run well to the finish. The desired end is the fullness of joy at God's right hand. It is eternal life.

---

[9] Thomas Schreiner, *Run to Win the Prize: Perseverance in the New Testament*, Kindle edition, 497.

A contrast for the community (:9)

They must beware of joining others in following the false teachers on a pathway that would reveal that they do not have God. The Spirit of God, through John, describes this in a very interesting way.

Everyone who goes on ahead and does not abide in the teaching of Christ. The NASB has *who goes too far.* They go beyond the teaching of Christ, the teaching that came from Christ and was proclaimed by the Apostles.

Imagine being on a large piece of property surrounded by a fence. All along the fence are warning signs, "Proceed beyond this point, and you are on damnable ground." These people go on ahead. They move outside the boundaries of the teaching of Christ. They may do it in the name of going forward and discovering "new things." They may do it in the name of some special source of revelation, or in some other way, but the moment they move outside of the apostles' doctrine concerning Jesus, they have crossed the line onto damnable soil. The people who can do that, and who do that, are people who do not have God. God's people are identified by where they stay, by where their loyalty is.

In his first letter, John told where false teachings come from.

1 John 4:1 *Beloved, do not believe every spirit, but test the spirits to see whether they are from God, for many false prophets have gone out into the world. ² By this you know the Spirit of God: every spirit that confesses that Jesus Christ has come in the flesh is from God, ³ and every spirit that does not confess Jesus is not from God. This is the spirit of the antichrist, which you heard was coming and now is in the world already.*

Is it possible for someone who is truly converted to depart from the teachings of Christ and to stay gone? The passage in 1 John 4 answers that.

⁴ Little children, you are from God and have overcome them, for he who is in you is greater than he who is in the world. ⁵ They are from the world; therefore they speak from the world, and the world listens to them. ⁶ We are from God. Whoever knows God listens to us; whoever is not from God does not listen to us. By this we know the Spirit of truth and the spirit of error.

He says that *you*, the children of God, *have overcome them*, the false prophets or false teachers, because the Holy Spirit who is in you is *greater than* [the evil spirit] *who is in the world.*

See also 1 John 2:18-19, which points out that the "antichrists" *went out from us* but were never really *of us*, because they did not continue *with us*. False prophets and false teachers seem to start well, but where they end up reveals that they were never really saved. In the church, we have human teachers, but we also have a divine Teacher, the Holy Spirit.

Returning to our text, *Everyone who goes on ahead and does not abide in the teaching of Christ, does not have God. Whoever abides in the teaching has both the Father and the Son.*

Genuine believers have the Spirit of God, the Spirit of truth. God brought you into the truth. He will keep you in the truth. Those who have the Spirit of God listen to John and the other apostles, and they heed God's warnings. Whoever abides in the teaching (of Christ) has the Father and the Son. They have eternal life and heed the warning signs, staying within the boundaries of the truth concerning Jesus.

A COOPERATION WITHIN TRUTH AND LOVE SETS THE BOUNDARY FOR THE CHURCH'S PARTICIPATION IN MINISTRY (:10-11)

As we've seen, truth and love set the boundaries for our understanding of who does have salvation and who is in the church. They also set the boundaries concerning whom we may assist in ministry while still be honoring God.

The believer's response to those who depart (:10)

When someone needs assistance to do their "ministry" and they don't represent the biblical Jesus and the biblical gospel, **you don't help them.** In the first century, these teachers traveled around and needed accommodations in order carry out their goals.

But, equally important, **you don't leave them or others with the impression that you agree with them.** John says you can't even give them a greeting—you don't treat them as though you and they are on the same team. Don't say, "Blessing to you!" (so to speak). Remember that God's Word never teaches us to respond hatefully. Be civil, kind, and mannerly.

It is amazing and sad to see how modern evangelicalism has intellectualized and emotionalized its way into granting legitimacy to teachers and movements of doctrine that are truly damnable. Too often, we practice a kind of love that Scripture doesn't recognize. It is deemed unsophisticated to use the forthrightness that has always characterized true men of God. The prophets and the apostles are not vague about what the truth is.

The reason for the believer's response to those who depart (:11)

We must not help them, leaving people confused about our differences. Lending them any credibility, is to have a part in their work when they lead someone astray. If someone sees my example, gives them ear and is led astray, then I have had a part in their wicked works

In verses 7-11 we have seen:

- Love and truth are discerning.
- Love and truth define the community.
- Love and truth identify the ones who threaten souls.
- Love and truth draw the lines so that we do not assist the work of deceivers and antichrists.

We must not compromise with false teachers. We must not entertain them. We must not assist them in leading others astray. If standing for the truth means we lose our respectability, then so be it, because we want to hear "well done, faithful servant." What's at stake? The souls of men and women!

5
TRUE FELLOWSHIP
(2 John 12-13)

The beginnings and endings of these inspired New Testament letters are fascinating, because they are not only the perfect word of God but also a window into the life of the early church. They give us a glimpse into the relationships that existed between those first believers. We can observe how they thought of each other, spoke to each other, behaved toward and cared for each other. God put these words here for our spiritual good. These letters teach us what fellowship is and how it functions. The issue of fellowship among God's people is mentioned often today, but that doesn't mean it's understood very well.

Sincere churches in our day often have the mistaken idea that being faithful to Scripture means trying to reproduce a first-century culture. As we look at the Scripture's descriptions of how believers relate to one another, we're looking into a culture that's very different from ours. It is mostly agrarian and much less mobile. The day begins with sunrise and ends with sunset. In many cases, people are out in a field during the day, plowing, planting and reaping. They are watching over flocks. There is interaction in business and in communities, but it often flows out of that agrarian culture. There are no cars, no electricity, no computers, no global connectivity—and the list goes on and on. If we try to reproduce that world, we must go out of the modern world. Some groups, like the Amish, have tried to do that. There are some believers who want to escape the world in which God, in His sovereignty and providence, has placed them. We may have romantic ideas about times and places that existed long ago, but God is wiser than we are, and He placed us into the time in which we are meant to live. We aren't meant to live in the first century. Yet the commands and principles of Scripture transcend culture. They are valid in any time or place. God wants us to recognize the timeless principles in His word and apply those principles right in the midst of this culture.

The church **is** counter-cultural, because it is to be like Heaven, not like the world. We get confused, though, about how to implement God's ideas in our culture. As John closes this letter, let's examine four characteristics of true fellowship.

TRUE FELLOWSHIP IS SUPERNATURAL

We don't create fellowship. God has already done that. True fellowship is the result of salvation. Fellowship is a partnership that involves a sharing of what we have in common. As we come to know Jesus as Lord, this fellowship exists in God. We have our introduction into the love that is known in the Trinity.

John 17: 14 *I have given them your word, and the world has hated them because they are not of the world, just as I am not of the world. ¹⁵ I do not ask that you take them out of the world, but that you keep them from the evil one. ¹⁶* **They are not of the world, just as I am not of the world.** *¹⁷ Sanctify them in the truth; your word is truth. ¹⁸ As you sent me into the world, so I have sent them into the world. ¹⁹ And for their sake I consecrate myself, that they also may be sanctified in truth. ²⁰ "I do not ask for these only, but also for those who will believe in me through their word, ²¹ that they may all be one, just as you, Father, are in me, and I in you, that they also may be in us, so that the world may believe that you have sent me. ²² The glory that you have given me I have given to them, that they may be one even as we are one, ²³ I in them and you in me, that they may become perfectly one, so that the world may know that you sent me and loved them even as you loved me.*

This passage from John's gospel tells us that oneness is found in the glory that we have received from Jesus (:22). It is a unity that shares in the oneness that is found in God (:21). It is a unity of identity found because of the divine nature. We share this fellowship with every true child of God, and it cannot possibly exist with unbelievers. Through salvation we have been separated from the rest of the world. It's not that we <u>shouldn't</u> have true fellowship with unbelievers, it's that we <u>don't</u>! So, we shouldn't be living like them!

Paul writes to the Corinthians:

2 Corinthians 6:14 *Do not be unequally yoked with unbelievers. For what partnership has righteousness with lawlessness? Or what fellowship has light with darkness?* ¹⁵ *What accord has Christ with Belial? Or what portion does a believer share with an unbeliever?* ¹⁶ *What agreement has the temple of God with idols? For we are the temple of the living God; as God said, "I will make my dwelling among them and walk among them, and I will be their God, and they shall be my people.* ¹⁷ *Therefore go out from their midst, and be separate from them, says the Lord, and touch no unclean thing; then I will welcome you,* ¹⁸ *and I will be a father to you, and you shall be sons and daughters to me, says the Lord Almighty."*

Notice the God-created division that now exists between believers and the rest of the world.

- Belief vs. unbelief
- Righteousness vs. lawlessness
- Light vs. darkness
- Jesus vs. Satan
- A *portion* that's an inheritance vs. a *portion* that's everlasting wrath
- The presence of the true God vs. paying tribute to false gods
- Fellowship with God vs. estrangement from God.
- God as Father vs. God as judge (vs.18)
- Cleanness vs. remaining in sin

Notice the repetition of words that speak of what fellowship really is: yoking together, partnership, fellowship, accord, portion-sharing together, and agreement. Looking at fellowship this way enables us to understand that **we** do not create it, nor is it superficial in nature like a dinner or a gathering. You are either in the fellowship or outside of it.

1 John 1:3 *that which we have seen and heard we proclaim also to you, so that you too may have fellowship with us; and indeed our fellowship is with the Father and with his Son Jesus Christ.*

1 John 1:6 *If we say we have fellowship with him while we walk in darkness, we lie and do not practice the truth.* ⁷ *But if we walk in the light, as he is in the light, we have fellowship with one another, and the blood of Jesus his Son cleanses us from all sin.*

1 Corinthians 1:9 *God is faithful, by whom you were called into the fellowship of his Son, Jesus Christ our Lord.*

This is the fellowship that John has with these two ladies or churches mentioned in 2 John 1 and 13. (See the first chapter of this commentary.) Both ladies are referred to as elect. He loves them and their children in the truth, and everyone who knows the truth loves them. They all share in truth forever. There is no doubt that they know the grace, mercy and peace that come from God the Father and from His Son, Jesus Christ. John commands them to love each other and to walk in truth. Later, he distinguishes them from the deceivers and antichrists.

From beginning to end the relationships expressed in this letter are **salvation relationships.** It is because of salvation that he shares such a relationship with these people, and they share such a relationship with others. They are elect sisters. True fellowship is a supernatural reality that flows from salvation.

TRUE FELLOWSHIP IS PRINCIPLED

Salvation has joined them together, and the truth and love of Jesus Christ rule over their relationship. Since it is a salvation relationship, it is scripturally informed and regulated. John has appealed to them and exhorted them with spiritual authority. True fellowship doesn't leave the truth of God out of its interactions.

That does not mean, of course, that every conversation between believers involves the quotation of Scripture. Instead, it means that in all our daily interactions, we have complete agreement on who and what is the final authority in our lives. We are the people of God, and the Word of God is the standard for our lives. It gives us a common and solid ground. We share a common life, and we share a common authority for mutual encouragement, correction, counsel, and care. This is important on a very practical level. It reminds us that for the child of God who really understands what fellowship is, nothing is more important than the truth of God's Word. Our fellowship is a fellowship in the truth.

- In this fellowship, we practice the truth (1 John 1:6).
- In this fellowship, we help each other materially, because we know it pleases God (Hebrews 13:16).
- In this fellowship, we share in the sufferings of Jesus (Philippians 3:10).
- This is the fellowship of the Spirit (Philippians 2:1).
- It is a partnership in the gospel (Philippians 1:5).
- It is a partnership in ministry (Galatians 2:9).

- It is sharing in the life of the church, such as at the Lord's Table (1 Corinthians 10:16), or when the church is gathered together (Acts 2:42).

In all these instances, truth is at the forefront. When someone says, "Well, we don't see eye to eye with that church's pulpit ministry, but our friends are there," or "It's more convenient for us," they immediately betray the fact that their concept of fellowship is not truth-centered. They don't understand the fellowship as found in the pages of Scripture. Wherever true fellowship is, the basis for it is the Word of God.

TRUE FELLOWSHIP IS PERSONAL AND WARM

True fellowship is a sharing that is found in salvation. Although Christian fellowship is informed and regulated by Scripture, this letter makes very clear that it is anything but formal, impersonal, and cold.

John desires to speak to them face to face. In Greek it's στόμα πρὸς στόμα (stoma pros stoma) and means mouth to mouth. He knows the love he feels for them is mutual.

I hope to come to you and talk face to face, so that our joy may be complete.

Personal affection, warmth in relationships, is throughout the New Testament. Here Paul describes his relationship to the Thessalonian believers:

1 Thessalonians 2:7 *But we were gentle among you, like a nursing mother taking care of her own children. ⁸ So, being affectionately desirous of you, we were ready to share with you not only the gospel of God but also our own selves, because you had become very dear to us. ⁹ For you remember, brothers, our labor and toil: we worked night and day, that we might not be a burden to any of you, while we proclaimed to you the gospel of God. ¹⁰ You are witnesses, and God also, how holy and righteous and blameless was our conduct toward you believers. ¹¹ For you know how, like a father with his children, ¹² we exhorted each one of you and encouraged you and charged you to walk in a manner worthy of God, who calls you into his own kingdom and glory.*

Paul speaks of Timothy as a son:

Philippians 2:22 *But you know Timothy's proven worth, how as a son with a father he has served with me in the gospel.*

When you come into the fellowship of salvation, you gain a family.

Mark 10:29 *Jesus said, "Truly, I say to you, there is no one who has left house or brothers or sisters or mother or father or children or lands, for my sake and for the gospel,* *30 who will not receive a hundredfold now in this time, houses and brothers and sisters and mothers and children and lands, with persecutions, and in the age to come eternal life."*

It's vitally important that we understand how fellowship functions. The Christian's responsibility before God involves multiple circles of responsibility. What is true for life in the church, for example, does not destroy what is true for life in the family. Nor does what is true for life in the family destroy what is true for life in the church.

Some people use their family relationships to disregard their responsibilities with respect to the church. Others focus so much on Christian fellowship that they neglect their families. We must learn to be faithful in both the realm of the family and the realm of the church, seeking wisdom from God to properly apply the scriptures to both. Often, we will struggle to find that balance. This is an area where we need to help each other grow in living out God's word faithfully. Some of us need to be encouraged to spend more time with brothers and sisters in Christ outside our own families. Others of us need to be encouraged to go home.

TRUE FELLOWSHIP IS SUBMISSIVE

John hopes to speak with them face to face. It is no doubt his intention and his expectation, but he knows he can't be certain. Both his future and theirs are in the hand of God. Because he trusts God with the future, he can be patient and can submit his desires to the sovereignty of God. True fellowship takes place in submission to the will of our God. Where we go, where we serve, how long we serve there, is all subject to the sovereign providences of our God. We must hold our Christian friendships with a kingdom perspective, not only in how we relate to each other but even when we can relate to each other in a personal way. The church will always be a place of transitions. The eternal state is the *only* place where we never have to say goodbye.

So, as we've looked through this window into the fellowship of the first-century church, we've learned that true fellowship…

- Exists in salvation
- Is guided by God's Word

- Is personal and warm
- Is enjoyed face to face, only as the Lord wills.

If you have the privilege of spending time with believers in other countries, you meet Christian people who don't even speak your language. But as you get to know them, there's an immediate bond because of your shared love of the God of the Bible, your shared love for the Lord Jesus Christ, your shared love for the Word of God.

Christian fellowship is a supernatural reality. We didn't create it. We just get to live in it due to our God's grace and mercy. Each of us should give God great thanks for our Christian brothers and sisters, loving one another sincerely from the heart in a way that is submissive to truth.

But if you don't know that fellowship, even if you're a Bible scholar, your need is to be saved. God has made the way for your sins to be forgiven and for you to enter into this Trinitarian love. That way is a person—Jesus, Who died for sinners like you. He's been raised from the dead, and He saves forever everyone who comes to Him with an honest heart. Come to him, knowing that you're a sinner who cannot save yourself. Look to Him and Him alone for a right standing with God. We declare these things so that you can have fellowship with Him and with us.

6
PEOPLE OF THE TRUTH
(3 John 1-8)

The little book of 3 John is a personal letter from the Apostle John to a Christian man named Gaius (:1), whom John loves as one of his children (:1, 4). In our day, the church tends to forget 3 John except for verse 2, which they misinterpret as a guarantee that God always wants us to be healthy and wealthy.

In the opening portion of the book of 3 John, we are reminded of the importance of truth. We <u>find the word *truth* five times in the first eight verses.</u>

Verse 1: *The elder to the beloved Gaius, whom I love in* **truth**.
Verse 3: *For I rejoiced greatly when the brothers came and testified to your* **truth***, as indeed you are walking in the* **truth***.*
Verse 4: *I have no greater joy than to hear that my children are walking in the* **truth***.*
Verse 8: *Therefore we ought to support people like these, that we may be fellow workers for the* **truth***.*

Truth is mentioned yet again in verse 12.

THERE IS TRUTH

There is truth as opposed to opinion and as opposed to error. It is a fixed standard by which everything else is measured and found to be right or found to be wanting. There is that which is substantive, concrete, and sure, that which accords with reality. Not every idea is equal.

God is the determiner, standard, and revealer of truth. It is <u>His</u> truth. When He saves people, He transfers them <u>into the truth</u>. Since the Fall, all men are born into a kingdom of moral and intellectual darkness. It's a kingdom of lies. When God saves people, He delivers them from the realm of darkness and lies, and brings them into the truth. They are transferred from the father of all lies to having God as their Father, the God of all truth. <u>He forms the church by the truth and for the truth.</u> As we begin looking at the small letter of 3 John, let's review the amazing relationship between the church, the gospel, and the truth.

The gospel is the word of truth.

Colossians 1:5 … *the hope laid up for you in heaven. Of this you have heard before in the word of the truth, the gospel, 6 which has come to you, as indeed in the whole world it is bearing fruit and increasing—as it also does among you, since the day you heard it and understood the grace of God in truth…*

The church stands for that truth and proclaims that truth.

2 Corinthians 4:2 *But we have renounced disgraceful, underhanded ways. We refuse to practice cunning or to tamper with God's word, but by the <u>open statement of the truth</u> we would commend ourselves to everyone's conscience in the sight of God.*

Not only do we proclaim the truth, but we proclaim it in a truthful manner. We don't use *disgraceful, underhanded ways.* We're not manipulative. We offer only the *open*, plain-spoken *statement* of God's Word. That's how the ministry of the Word of God is to take place.

1 Timothy 3:15 …*if I delay, you may know how one ought to behave in the household of God, which is the church of the living God, <u>a pillar and buttress of the truth</u>.*

Where can someone find the truth? It's in the Lord's church. We are meant to display the truth and to uphold the truth. The people of God are described as **people of the truth.**

John 18:37 *Then Pilate said to him, "So you are a king?" Jesus answered, "You say that I am a king. For this purpose I was born and for this purpose I have come into the world—to bear witness to the truth. Everyone who is <u>of the truth</u> listens to my voice."*

By God's grace, we have heard the voice of the Son of God and have been saved. Now each of us is among those who are *of the truth* and who have *come to the knowledge of the truth:*

1 Tim 2:3 *This is good, and it is pleasing in the sight of God our Savior, ⁴ who desires all people to be saved and to come to the <u>knowledge of the truth</u>.*

False teachers are deprived of the truth and abide in darkness.

1 Tim 6:3 *If anyone teaches a different doctrine and does not agree with the sound words of our Lord Jesus Christ and the teaching that accords with godliness, ⁴ he is puffed up with conceit and understands nothing. He has an unhealthy craving for controversy and for quarrels about words, which produce envy, dissension, slander, evil suspicions, ⁵ and constant friction among people who are depraved in mind and <u>deprived of the truth</u>, imagining that godliness is a means of gain.*

False doctrine is teaching that is deprived of the truth. Though it arrives claiming to be the truth, it's without the truth.

God's truth has formed the community of the saints and abides there.

2 John 1:1 *The elder to the elect lady and her children, whom I love in truth, and not only I, but also all who know the truth, ² because of the truth that abides in us and will be with us forever:*

In 3 John, the apostle is emphasizing truth in the context of a personal letter. John wrote something for the church, but a man by the name of Diotrephes has stood in the way of that communication. His resistance, however, does not block John's relationship with his dear friend Gaius. John writes to him giving thanks for the good reports he has heard about him walking in truth. That brings joy to the heart of the aged Apostle John. He's writing to encourage Gaius in the pathway he's been walking, but he is also writing to communicate a warning through Gaius. This warning concerning Diotrephes would inform and encourage the faithful in the Lord's church. <u>So, the letter contains both encouragement and warnings, and it communicates assurances for those who are faithful.</u> We're getting a glimpse into how the truth operates in the lives of God's people, even on a casual level—in the midst of a friendship or a personal letter.

A large portion of what John has to say has to do with hospitality. We'll deal with that in the next chapter, but what is especially emphasized in the first 8 verses is that the people of God are a people of truth.

This is how you identify God's people.

The people of God are identified by their relationship to the truth as it is in Jesus Christ. They are identified not by traditions, not by cultural preferences, not by social or political concerns but by **truth**. <u>They love the One who IS the truth</u>, the Lord Jesus Christ. <u>They love the Word of God</u>. As Jesus told us in John 17, the Word of God *is truth* and <u>God's people love their brothers and sisters</u> who are *of the truth*.

That relationship to truth is made plain not just by words but by deeds.

As John writes to Gaius, we learn three important lessons about this fellowship of truth as we simply pay attention to what *the elder, the presbyter*, has to say to his beloved friend. (Remember that John is the last surviving apostle. He is not just "an elder." He is *the elder*. He is the most revered servant of God in the Lord's church at this time.)

In studying this passage, we not only learn how the truth operates among God's people; we may have some misconceptions corrected at the same time. Truth's operation in the life of the church is often misunderstood. These verses speak to us concerning the love that exists in the truth, the joy that exists in the truth, and the partnership that exists in the truth.

LOVE EXISTS IN TRUTH (:1-2)

:1 *The elder to the beloved Gaius, whom I love in truth. Beloved, I pray that all may go well with you and that you may be in good health, as it goes well with your soul.*

The people of truth are also the people of love. Where truth is truly found, love will be present. Genuine love is not accidentally present where the truth is known. Because the truth is known, having broken into a life and burst upon the mind and the heart, <u>holy love</u> is present.

<u>God is the giver of truth and the teacher of truth. The same God who brings people into the truth, brings people into His love.</u>

God is the One who saves, and He is the giver of truth and of love. So, when He saved us, He brought us into the truth. As He brought us into the truth, He also brought us into His love. In fact, we share in the love that has forever been known in the Trinity.

Salvation is a spiritual miracle. Deliverance from darkness and entrance into the truth is a supernatural work of God, and the love that is present there is salvation's love. As God's people, we share in a common love, because we share in a common salvation. We have love for the Father, love for the Son, and love of the Spirit. We love God's offspring, our brothers and sisters in the faith. We love the truth. We love righteousness. These are new loves resulting from salvation. We even have a love for the lost, a burden for those who don't yet know the Savior.

When the elder (John) writes to Gaius and says, "whom I love in truth," it could mean that he loves him sincerely. But the context of 3 John and of 2 John leads us to believe that he means that his love for Gaius is found in, and exists in, the truth. That's the kind of love we know as believers in the Lord Jesus. It's a mark of salvation.

2 John 1:1 *The elder to the elect lady and her children, whom I love in truth, and not only I, <u>but also all who know the truth</u>, ² because of the truth that abides in us and will be with us forever...*

Everyone who knows the truth loves those who share the same salvation, are God's children, and are walking in truth.

1 John 3:10 *By this it is evident who are the children of God, and who are the children of the devil: whoever does not practice righteousness is not of God, nor is the one who does not <u>love his brother</u>.*

1 John 3:14 *We know that we have passed out of death into life, because <u>we love the brothers</u>. Whoever does not love abides in death.*

1 John 4:8 *Anyone who <u>does not love</u> does not know God, because God is love.*

1 John 4:20 *If anyone says, "I love God," and hates his brother, he is a liar; for he who does not <u>love his brother</u> whom he has seen cannot love God whom he has not seen.*

God's people love, and they love because they are in the truth, and this love is of the truth.

1 John 5:20 *And we know that the Son of God has come and has given us understanding, so that <u>we may know him who is true</u>; and <u>we are in him who is true</u>, in his Son Jesus Christ. He is the <u>true God</u> and eternal life.*

John is able to write of his love for Gaius and to make clear that it is a love that exists because of the truth. Notice that where this gospel love exists, there are two realms of concern.

LOVE IN TRUTH IS CONCERNED ABOUT THE SOUL

John has received a report about his friend. He has received this report from some traveling missionaries (we will look at this more later). He has heard that Gaius is doing well spiritually. As he will make plain in verses 3 and 4, there is no area of another person's life that John is more concerned with.

This is the chief concern of someone who is walking in the love that exists in truth: How is your soul? How are you doing spiritually? It is disappointing to a pastor when people claim that they know Jesus Christ as Lord and Savior, and claim that they love another person, and yet it is painfully obvious that their definition of love doesn't make the person's soul their primary concern. The most important thing about anyone's life is, are they truly born again? Do they know the Lord? If they know the Lord, how are they doing spiritually? That's primary. For a parent who's walking in truth and love, the number one concern for their children is their spiritual condition, not merely getting homework done and getting to extracurricular activities. In the realm of friendship, your friend's spiritual condition is your number one concern. As a church member, when you engage someone on social media, your number one concern should be the condition of their soul. Many people claim to be walking in the love of God, but they value popularity and camaraderie more than the spiritual wellbeing of the person they say they love.

But notice that John's love and concern for this man doesn't stop with the condition of his soul. John prays for the prosperity of this man in every realm.

LOVE IN TRUTH CARES ABOUT THE WHOLE PERSON

True love does not ignore material realities. John expresses a concern about Gaius's health. John expresses concern about Gaius's entire life. It would include his business matters, the plans he was engaged in, his relationships, and every other realm of his life.

God's love doesn't make us insensitive to temporal realities. Yes, our first concern is for people's souls, but it's not our only concern. Because we love them, we're concerned about the whole person, the whole life.

1 John 3:16 *By this we know love, that he laid down his life for us, and we ought to lay down our lives for the brothers.* ¹⁷ *But if anyone* <u>*has the world's goods*</u> *and sees his brother in need, yet closes his heart against him, how does God's love abide in him?* ¹⁸ *Little children, let us not love in word or talk but in deed and in truth.*

James 2:15 *If a brother or sister is poorly clothed and lacking in daily food,* ¹⁶ *and one of you says to them, "Go in peace, be warmed and filled," without giving them the things needed for the body, what good is that?*

This corrects the common misconception that truth is cold. <u>Truth is not cold.</u> Gaius is described as *beloved.* Gaius is loved by God and therefore loved by John. If our concept of loving truth does not include our loving people, we have misunderstood the truth.

JOY EXISTS IN TRUTH (:3-4)

Our concerns determine our celebrations. If we really care about something, then when we see a person we love doing well in that area, we celebrate. So, we not only see that <u>love</u> exists in the realm of truth, we see that <u>joy</u> exists in the realm of truth. This joy involves the truth—and it's no small joy. If your greatest concern for a person is the condition of their soul, then you will have no greater desire for a person than to know that they are walking in the truth, and your greatest joy will be when that happens. Tell us what you celebrate the most, what brings you the most joy, and we can show you what are your greatest concerns.

When the people you love walk in the truth, it is a reason for great rejoicing.

John says, *For I rejoiced greatly....* That's a superlative adverb. He says, *Greatly I rejoiced when the brothers came and testified to your truth.* This was John's attitude about all his spiritual offspring. The report of Gaius walking in the truth brought delight, even though John didn't personally witness it. Notice verse 4, *I have no greater joy than to hear that my children are walking in the truth.*

When the people you love walk in the truth, it is noticed by others.

In the case of Gaius, his walk in the truth was shining forth in a way that people who were strangers to him were able to bring news of this to John. He was able to celebrate Gaius's walk in the truth, because someone else recognized it and reported about it.

When people who are in the truth and care about the truth witness their loved ones walking in the truth, it matters greatly to them.

John wrote, *I rejoiced greatly.* He wrote, *I have no greater joy.* We can each ask ourselves, Can I say that? Is there <u>nothing</u> that matters more to me than to see the people I care about walking in the truth of God's Word? Is there <u>nothing</u> that moves my heart so greatly? With my children or with my friends or at work or as a church member, where are my celebrations focused? What do I celebrate joyfully?

1. Note that it is a walk in **truth.**
2. Note that it is a **walk** in truth.

This corrects another misconception. <u>Truth is not stoic</u>. Some people associate doctrinal faithfulness with an approach to God that is emotionally stifled, with worship that is emotionally empty. They try so hard not to be emotionalists that their worship is emotionally empty. That's not what we see in Scripture. There is a difference between emotion and emotionalism. Emotionalism is not spiritually healthy. It is dangerous. Truth is to reign over our emotions, but when truth is reigning over the emotions, it doesn't make us numb. In fact, it stimulates emotions. There are things that we rejoice over and celebrate that we would not otherwise think about. God's truth activates both new love and a new kind of joy. When people encounter you, or encounter your church, they should encounter a supernatural joy that is activated by truth.

THE PARTNERSHIP THAT EXISTS IN TRUTH (:5-8)

We have seen the love and joy that exist in truth. Now we see one specific area of Gaius' truth walk where John wants to give affirmation and exhortation, his support of traveling missionaries. He has supported preachers of the gospel by showing hospitality to them, and those same men have now arrived in John's presence and given a testimony of how Gaius has ministered to them.

What Gaius has done

In the first century, hospitality is not just a nice thing to do. It is a necessity. Travel is full of dangers and inconveniences. Often, public places to stay are both dangerous and unfit. Travelers are dependent on those they know, maybe alliances formed along family lines or friendship. The host will provide needed food, shelter and safety. It is a cultural virtue, but also a Christian duty. God's love demands it for your brethren. Missionaries teaching the

Word of God are dependent upon the hospitality of believers to give them a place to stay, a place to be fed, a place to be safe. Both the Old and New Testaments are full of examples of hospitality. Gaius has been practicing it. We learn in verses 9-10 that a man in the church named Diotrephes has been refusing that kind of hospitality. Gaius has not been influenced by that, but has opened his home, his life, and his resources to help these men.

- He has demonstrated love (:6).
- This love has been noticed by the church (:6)
- This demonstration of love has required effort (:5).

Beloved, it is a faithful thing you do in all your <u>*efforts*</u> *for these brothers.* The word ἐργάσῃ (ergasē) translated *efforts* is related to the word for work or labor. As we'd say it, he has "put himself out" to help these men.

He has shown love for brothers whom he had not known personally (:5). His hospitality has been supernatural and principled. These are men who are doing ministry (:7). They are taking the gospel of Jesus Christ, refusing any kind of support from pagans. They would trust in God's provision for them through God's people.

John gives three reasons why Gaius's hospitality is good.

a. These brothers are <u>doctrinally sound</u>. They have gone out *for the sake of the name* of the Lord Jesus. They truly represent the gospel. These are sound brothers. That's a good reason for him to support them.

b. They have been <u>financially in need</u>. They have gone out *for the sake of the name, accepting nothing from the Gentiles.* In other words, they have carried out their ministry in a way that will not bring reproach on the name of the Lord Jesus, not wanting their motives to be misunderstood. By not accepting anything from the pagans, they do not put a stumbling block in the way of the gospel. If their needs are to be met, God's people must do it. That's very much like the ministry of the Apostle Paul, which these men are mirroring, so this is a second good reason to support them.

c. These men are <u>partners in the gospel</u>, *fellow workers for the truth.* (:8) They are advancing and proclaiming the truth. They are instruments of God to see people brought into the realm of the truth through salvation. Gaius, or anyone who helps such people, becomes a fellow worker for the truth. People look at our giving in the church and think it's crazy. They wonder why you take your hard-earned money and give it in the name of ministry. You do it because you know the truth. You've been brought into the truth. You understand that the church is the pillar and support of the truth. By supporting those who proclaim the truth, you know that you have a part in their work.

His care for them has been tangible and honorable (:6) When John says, *you will do well*, it's a way of asking him to please continue doing this. As Gaius encounters people like this, John wants him to send them on their way in a way that fits Gaius's reverence for God, treating them as he would treat the Lord. That means his help for them was not minimalistic, but robust and sacrificial.

How John characterizes what Gaius has done

- It is faithfulness (:5)—Faithful both in the sense that it is in keeping with what God would want, and in the sense that it's full of faith, reflecting a belief in the truth.
- It is well-doing (:6)—It's commendable and right.
- It is worthy of God (:6)—Something that glorifies and pleases God.
- It is something God's people ought to do (:8).
- It is a partnership in the truth (:8).

When people walk in the truth, the truth shines in their lives in tangible ways that reflect both beliefs and practice.

This corrects another misconception. Truth is not isolated and uncooperative. It's not longing for a fight. Instead, as people of the truth, we long for the advancement of the truth, and we help and support others who are workers for the truth. We welcome them, support them, and send them on their way blessed.

What do you find in those people who belong to the truth?

- You find the love that exists because of the truth.
- You find new concerns and new celebrations.
- You find new joy, and the greatest joy is when the people you love really walk in the truth.
- You find a new priority, the advancement of the truth.

- You find the partnership that demonstrates the fellowship of the truth.

There **is** truth in this world. Rejoice that you're a part of the people of the truth. Thank God for taking you from the domain of darkness, where you were a slave to the father of lies. Thank Him for transferring you into the kingdom of His dear Son, into the kingdom of truth and love. Ask Him to make the advancement of truth your joy, your walk and your goal.

7
TRUTH MODELS
(3 John 9-15)

God designed us to learn things first by imitating models, and also by instruction in words. Children imitate their parents, but imitation doesn't stop with childhood. As adults, we continue learning this way. A person can try to explain skiing, but you'll learn much better when someone stays with you to demonstrate and guide you.

The same is true in the church. We're meant to preach and teach the Word of God, and we're also to live it. God's people learn what it means to live the Christian life not just by what they hear, but also by what they see. We need models, and God calls each of us to be one. In this way truth is passed on from one life to the next and from one generation to another. <u>People need to be taught the truth by example</u>. In fact, of the eight references to imitation in the New Testament, all but one mention imitating people. The one exception is in Ephesians.

Ephesians 5:1 *Therefore <u>be imitators of God</u>, as beloved children.*

Every other reference to imitation in the New Testament includes imitating people:

2 Thessalonians 3:7 *For you yourselves know how you ought to <u>imitate us</u>, because we were not idle when we were with you, ⁸ nor did we eat anyone's bread without paying for it, but with toil and labor we worked night and day, that we might not be a burden to* *any of you.* [9] *It was not because we do not have that right, but <u>to give you in ourselves an example to imitate.</u>*

Hebrews 13:7 *Remember your leaders, those who spoke to you the word of God. Consider the outcome of their way of life, and <u>imitate their faith.</u>*

1 Corinthians 4:16 *I urge you, then, <u>be imitators of me.</u>*

1 Corinthians 11:1 <u>*Be imitators of me,*</u> *as I am of Christ.*

1 Thessalonians 1:6 *And you <u>became imitators of us and of the Lord,</u> for you received the word in much affliction, with the joy of the Holy Spirit...*

1 Thessalonians 2:14 *For you, brothers, <u>became imitators of the churches of God in Christ Jesus that are in Judea.</u> For you suffered the same things from your own countrymen as they did from the Jews...*

Hebrews 6:11 *And we desire each one of you to show the same earnestness to have the full assurance of hope until the end,* [12] *so that you may not be sluggish, <u>but imitators of those who through faith and patience inherit the promises.</u>*

We saw in the last chapter that the people of God are a people of truth. They also are a people who learn the truth and pass it on both by word and by deed. We need models and we need to <u>be</u> models.

In this passage (3 John 9-15), John talks about the importance of making the right choices in the realm of imitation. Gaius has conducted himself in a way that is worthy of imitation. John is now concerned that he stay on that pathway. He does not want him dissuaded from it by the bad example, or by the intimidating pressure of others. To that end, he now exhorts Gaius to imitate what is good and to reject what is evil.

A PROBLEM TO BE ADDRESSED (:9-10)

In this letter to Gaius, John has shown that in the truth there is love, there is joy, and there is partnership in ministry. Traveling missionaries have reported to John that Gaius has exhibited all of this, and John has rejoiced. Now he turns his attention to a problem that Gaius must have encountered.

Diotrephes, a man with authority in a church, is exhibiting the opposite of everything good that John has heard about Gaius. John does not want Gaius to be influenced by him.

- Gaius exhibits love— Diotrephes does not.
- Gaius exhibits hospitality— Diotrephes does not.
- Gaius supports ministers of the gospel— Diotrephes does not.
- Gaius exhibits love for the truth and submission to the truth— Diotrephes does not.
- Gaius is worthy of praise— Diotrephes is not.

Diotrephes is an immediate problem.

Incidentally, there are always those who point out problems in churches and think we need to re-create the first-century church because it was "pure" and "pristine". Other people consider leaving their particular church because it has problems. The truth is, as you look at the various books of the New Testament, you find that there were problems in churches from the earliest times. The church must deal with problems for a host of reasons:

- Saved people are not yet glorified.
- The church is the object of Satanic attack.
- There are people who profess faith in Christ who are not really saved, so we deal with unbelievers in the midst of the church.
- Genuine believers need to grow in the Christian faith. Even faithful believers have sinful moments and seasons of struggle.

Paul was able to say, *there must be factions among you in order that those who are genuine among you may be recognized* (1 Cor 11:19). God allows divisions so that those who are genuine may become evident and so that His people will grow. Problems in the church are not new, and in this letter, John is dealing with one.

A message resisted

John wrote a letter for the church, and Diotrephes resisted it. We don't know what church it was nor what kind of letter it was. It is unlikely that it was 2 John. We don't know for certain that this was even the church where Gaius belonged. (Verse 9 uses the third-person plural *them* instead of the second-person plural *you*.) Further, we don't know how Diotrephes resisted this letter. Did he confiscate it? Destroy it? Dispute what John wrote? We don't know. But here is what we do know.

A man rebelling

Diotrephes is rebellious. He has often been described in terms of his abuse
of authority and love for authority, but if this is all we see, then we have
missed his true character. The basic problem with him is that he resists
authority. To put it in modern business terms, Diotrephes is a middle
manager who has no regard for the authority over him. John writes, *He does
not acknowledge our authority.* Diotrephes feels free to resist apostolic authority,
so it's no wonder that he abuses authority when he's over others.

No one should ever be in a position of spiritual authority who hasn't
demonstrated that he is committed to submitting to authority. People who
abuse authority have no respect for authority. They have no respect for God's
authority, and those who do not respect God's authority will not submit to
legitimate human authority. These things go hand in hand, because God is
the one who has ordained authority in human relationships and societal
structures. Anyone who has authority is also under God's authority.
Whatever authority we exercise, we must do it fearfully, submissively and
humbly, for the glory of God.

He does not acknowledge apostolic authority

The verse literally reads, *he does not receive us.* John uses the word ἐπιδέχομαι
(epidechomai). The standard Greek lexicon[10] offers two meanings for this
word.

    a.   to receive into one's presence in a friendly manner, *receive,
       welcome* τινὰ *someone*).
    b.   to acknowledge receptively, *accept*=not reject.

There is no evidence in the context that John has attempted to visit the
church he speaks of, so the most likely meaning is the second. Diotrephes
does not receive them in the sense that he does not acknowledge them
receptively. He rejects them in the sense that he rejects John and his

---

[10] William Arndt, Frederick W. Danker, and Walter Bauer, *A Greek-English Lexicon
of the New Testament and Other Early Christian Literature* (Chicago: University of
Chicago Press, 2000), 370.

representatives. He rejects apostolic authority. That's how the ESV translators have taken it.

His pride does not allow his submission

Why would Diotrephes do this? Because he has a love for preeminence. Φιλοπρωτεύω (*philoproteuo*, from *phileo* meaning love, and *protos* meaning first). That is, he is proud. Because he is proud, he loves preeminence and will not submit to John's authority, which he despises. His rebellion manifests itself in two ways.

His rebellion is manifested in wicked words (accusation) (:10)

In verse 10, John says Diotrephes has been *talking wicked nonsense*. He has been saying wicked things that are not true, that *make no sense*. Notice that it is not nonsense in a general sense. It is nonsense in a targeted sense. He has manifested his rebellion *against us*, against God-ordained authority, by aiming his tongue at those who represent that authority.

His rebellion is manifested in evil deeds (:10)

His wickedness does not stop with his mouth. He's *not content with that*. His evil is seen in that he *refuses* to show the hospitality that would help those who preach the truth, and even worse, he *puts* people *out of the church* if they do show hospitality to godly brothers.

A PRINCIPLE TO BE APPLIED (:11)

In order to combat this, John reminds Gaius of a principle by giving him an imperative in verse 11. *Beloved, do not imitate evil but imitate good. Whoever does good is from God; whoever does evil has not seen God.* Note three things about this command.

A command that reflects love (*Beloved*)

All of God's commands are loving. They are <u>always</u> for our spiritual good. It's right to elevate the inerrancy and sufficiency of Scripture, but the Word of God is not only true—it is good. Since it's both, wisdom means your purpose in searching the Scriptures won't be to try to justify your point of view. You'll come submissively, searching the Scriptures for the truth, because all of God's truth is loving and good.

A command that requires discernment

The command requires discernment. Gaius must recognize evil and recognize good, and then set his gaze, his choices, on what is good. Scripture tells us how to identify the good: Have a mind and a life saturated with the truth of Scripture. Practice what the Bible teaches. As we do this, we begin to mature in our ability to recognize what's right and what's wrong.

Hebrews 5:12 *For though by this time you ought to be teachers, you need someone to teach you again the basic principles of the oracles of God. You need milk, not solid food,* *13 for everyone who lives on milk is unskilled in the word of righteousness, since he is a child. 14 But solid food is for the mature, for those who have their powers of discernment trained by constant practice to distinguish good from evil.*

In this quote from Hebrews, *solid food* refers to *the word of righteousness.* If someone knows the Word of God and then practices it, they'll grow in their ability *to distinguish good from evil.* Why is the church often so undiscerning? Because it's either not being taught the Scriptures, or not taking the next step, which is to live them out.

A command that remembers salvation

John also wants Gaius to remember that people who really know the Lord are characterized by doing good. People who are characterized by doing evil don't really know God. This relates to the matter of salvation. This truth operates on both sides of the imitation command.

- Those who do good are the result of God's saving work.
- Those who imitate the good are the result of God's saving work.

He says, *Whoever does good is from God.* This orientation to what is good comes from the new birth—from a new nature. It is salvation, explained by nothing less than God's own power. God makes people who pursue good and who desire to imitate what is good. God's saving work can be described in two ways.

- Salvation comes from God.
- Salvation results in spiritual sight.

He also says this: *Whoever does evil has not seen God.* That's spiritual blindness. That stings.

But the person who does good is from God and has seen God. That's salvation. The spiritual eyes have been opened. One is now able to see God by faith. They have come face to face through the truth, through the Word of God, with the true God. Now their life is characterized by a pursuit of what is good, an affection for those who do what is good, and a desire to follow those who do what is good.

A PERSON TO BE ADMIRED (:12)

So, the principle is this: Don't imitate the evildoer. Imitate the person who does what is good. John doesn't just give the principle. He now provides examples.

The example of John

First, John himself serves as an example. He writes, *and you know that our testimony is true.* It's as if he's reminding Gaius, "Hey, son, listen to me." Paul did something similar. He was not shy about teaching the churches to imitate him. He wrote, *Imitate me as I imitate Christ.* He's a Christ-follower and an apostle, so to call for people to follow him is to call them to follow Jesus. That is what we all desire, to follow Christ. John is not shy about this, either. He reminds Gaius and anyone who reads this letter, that it's a *testimony* that is *true.*

John shows both strength and godly restraint in this letter. His restraint is seen in that he doesn't condemn Diotrephes outright. He doesn't say, "Diotrephes is a false teacher, a heretic, a lost man, a devil." But John's strength is also seen, because he clearly states what the problem is, and the true nature of what Diotrephes is doing. John will not ignore what is happening. If he comes, he will *bring up what Diotrephes is doing.* Diotrephes's wrong actions will not be ignored. John is actually giving Diotrephes an opportunity to repent.

The example of Demetrius

Where John really puts the spotlight is on another man, Demetrius.

Who is he?

We don't know anything more about this man than what we have here. He could be the person who is carrying this letter to Gaius, or a leader in the church that Gaius belongs to, or one of the traveling teachers, the kind of man that Gaius and others should support. We don't know.

What are his credentials?

What we do know are the credentials that John mentions.

A consistent testimony from men

Demetrius *has received a good testimony from everyone*. His godliness is not in dispute. He's not sinless, but the pattern of his life is a consistent one across multiple spheres of influence.

A consistent testimony from truth

This testimony is not merely a subjective one. It's not just that people like him. His life reflects faithfulness to the Scriptures. The Bible itself, God's true Word, now gives its testimony to his life. That's a good question for us to consider. Would the Bible bear witness to the way that we are living?

A careful testimony from the apostle

John takes it a step further. He puts his own stamp of approval on this man. In these three ways, what John is saying to Gaius is essentially, "Stay on the pathway you're on. Keep living a life that gives joy to those who long to see their children walking in the truth. Keep your eyes on people who do what is good and right in the sight of God. Do not be persuaded by men like Diotrephes, but admire men like Demetrius."

A PATIENCE TO BE ATTAINED (:13-15)

As we finish our study of 3 John, notice that the apostle John is a model for us. In this letter, he is a particularly a model of patience. We see his patience in two ways.

Patience in a crisis (:10)

John shows patience during a crisis, one that involves him. Even in a crisis that's focused on other people, it is hard to be patient and calm. But in this case, words of *wicked nonsense* are being aimed at him. And yet, as we read what he says about it and how he plans to handle it, there is no sense of panic. Amazingly, John doesn't even seem certain that he will ever visit that church. Verse 10 may mean *when I come*, but either way, verse 14 says it's his *hope* (not certainty) that he will see Gaius soon. There's a problem to be dealt with, but there's no panic. Here is an aged, mature, godly man who understands that the church is not his. He is an under-shepherd of Jesus, the chief Shepherd.

John has learned that **because there is no panic in Heaven, there need not be panic on earth.** If panic is your default mindset, learn to rest in the Lord. Rest in Him without being negligent. Deal with issues but trust the Lord to work.

Patience in relationships and ministry (:13-15)

This same patience is shown in his personal relationships and ministry. He says he had *much to write* to Gaius, but he *would rather not write with pen and ink.* He would rather meet to discuss it. We don't know why he thought it could wait, or why he didn't want to write it, but he was willing to wait. He was not a captive of the tyranny of the urgent.[11] When needed, John could wait. Young leaders often struggle with this, thinking, "We have to deal with this now." But as you walk longer with Jesus and as you mature in the faith, you learn to rest in God's timing. You learn that not every situation should be dealt with now. In some cases, a better time will come in the future.

The very peace that John wishes to Gaius and the Christian friends is the peace that this man of God knows in his own heart and life. And it's the peace that we are called to walk in. We need truth models, and we need to model the truth for others.

As we close our study of 3 John, the examples of the apostle John, Gaius, and Demetrius speak to us, urging us to turn from every sin. By God's grace, we are to choose good examples and to set an example that is good and God-glorifying for all who are influenced by us.

---

[11] This phrase comes from Charles E. Hummel, *Tyranny of the Urgent* (Downers Grove, IL: IVP, 1967, Revised & enlarged edition, 2013).

8
CALLED, LOVED AND KEPT
(Jude 1-2)

The book of Jude has been described by more than one person as the most neglected book of the New Testament. Yet its message is urgently needed by the church because of what we face today and what we'll likely face in the future if the Lord should tarry.

Why is it often neglected? My friend Tom Schreiner's commentary on Jude offers three reasons. First, its **brevity**. It's only 25 verses. Perhaps we think that because it's brief, it's not important, so we don't spend much time in it. Second, its **strangeness**. Jude speaks of some things that are not easy to identify. Not only that, it also contains quotes from non-canonical writings: 1 Enoch and The Assumption of Moses. It's distinctly different from most of the New Testament letters, although it's very much like 2 Peter. Third, its **tone**.

"The message of Jude is alien to many in today's world, for Jude emphasized that the Lord will certainly judge evil intruders who are attempting to corrupt the church. The message of judgment strikes many in our world as intolerant, unloving, and contrary to the message of love proclaimed elsewhere in the New Testament. Nevertheless, this short letter should not be ignored. Some of the most beautiful statements about God's sustaining grace are found in Jude (vs. 24-25), and they shine with a greater brilliance when contrasted with the false teachers who had departed from the Christian faith. We can also say that the message of judgment is especially relevant to people today, for our churches are prone to sentimentality, suffer from moral breakdown, and too often fail to pronounce a definitive word of judgment because of an inadequate definition of love."[12]

We dare not neglect it. We face dangers similar to those the church faced in Jude's day, and our God gave us the book of Jude that we might know it and live in the light of it. Let's study it, beginning with the greeting. We will look at it under three headings—the author, the audience and the aim.

THE AUTHOR (:1)

He identifies himself as *Jude, a servant of Jesus Christ and brother of James*. The Hebrew form of his name is Judah, and in Greek it is Judas. It was a popular name at that time. A very famous Judas, Judas Maccabeus, had led in the Jewish revolt against Antiochus Epiphanes in the 160's B.C. He was considered one of the greatest warriors in Jewish history.

The translators of the English Bible, probably because of the name's association with Judas Iscariot, translated it *Jude*, and that practice continues to this day.

There are several men named Judas in the New Testament, but only one who is likely the author of this letter.

The Brother of Jesus and James

It is Judas, the half-brother of the Lord Jesus, and the brother of James.

The author identifies himself as *the brother of James*, and there is no further explanation of who he is or who his brother is. This indicates that these brothers were well known to the church, with such a reputation that people would recognize them.

We know that our Lord was virgin-born, but he had half-brothers and half-sisters, the offspring of Joseph and Mary.

Matt 13:54 *and coming to his hometown he taught them in their synagogue, so that they were astonished, and said, "Where did this man get this wisdom and these mighty works?*

---

[12] Schreiner, Thomas R., *New American Commentary: 1, 2 Peter, Jude: An Exegetical and Theological Exposition of Holy Scripture* (Nashville, B&H Publishing Group, 2003), p. 403

55 Is not this the carpenter's son? Is not his mother called Mary? And are not his brothers James and Joseph and Simon and Judas? 56 And are not all his sisters with us? Where then did this man get all these things?"

Mark 6:3 *Is not this the carpenter, the son of Mary and brother of James and Joses and Judas and Simon? And are not his sisters here with us?" And they took offense at him.*

Some scholars, including John Calvin, have identified this letter with the apostle Judas.

Luke 6:13 *And when day came, he called his disciples and chose from them twelve, whom he named apostles: 14 Simon, whom he named Peter, and Andrew his brother, and James and John, and Philip, and Bartholomew, 15 and Matthew, and Thomas, and James the son of Alphaeus, and Simon who was called the Zealot, 16 and Judas the son of James, and Judas Iscariot, who became a traitor.*

Note, however, that the apostle Judas was not the brother of James (despite what the KJV says)[13], but the Son of James.

Not a believer during our Lord's earthly ministry

This Judas (Jude), Jesus' half-brother, was not a believer during the time that our Lord was ministering on earth.

John 7:1 *After this Jesus went about in Galilee. He would not go about in Judea, because the Jews were seeking to kill him. 2 Now the Jews' Feast of Booths was at hand. 3 So his brothers said to him, "Leave here and go to Judea, that your disciples also may see the works you are doing. 4 For no one works in secret if he seeks to be known openly. If you do these things, show yourself to the world." 5 For not even his brothers believed in him.*

Mark describes an event just after Jesus appointed the Twelve.

---

[13] Literally, "Judas of James." See *International Critical Commentary* on Luke 6:16 for why this means "son of" instead of "brother of.". Tyndale, Coverdale, Cranmer and Luther interpreted this as "son of." Luke used the word for "brother" when he meant brother.

Mark 3:20-21 *Then he went home, and the crowd gathered again, so that they could not even eat. ²¹ And when his family heard it, they went out to seize him, for they were saying, "He is out of his mind."*

Became a believer by the time of Pentecost

In all likelihood, he became a believer after the resurrection of Christ. Note verse 14 of Acts 1.

Acts 1:6 *So when they had come together, they asked him, "Lord, will you at this time restore the kingdom to Israel?" ⁷ He said to them, "It is not for you to know times or seasons that the Father has fixed by his own authority. ⁸ But you will receive power when the Holy Spirit has come upon you, and you will be my witnesses in Jerusalem and in all Judea and Samaria, and to the end of the earth." ⁹ And when he had said these things, as they were looking on, he was lifted up, and a cloud took him out of their sight. ¹⁰ And while they were gazing into heaven as he went, behold, two men stood by them in white robes, ¹¹ and said, "Men of Galilee, why do you stand looking into heaven? This Jesus, who was taken up from you into heaven, will come in the same way as you saw him go into heaven." ¹² Then they returned to Jerusalem from the mount called Olivet, which is near Jerusalem, a Sabbath day's journey away. ¹³ And when they had entered, they went up to the upper room, where they were staying, Peter and John and James and Andrew, Philip and Thomas, Bartholomew and Matthew, James the son of Alphaeus and Simon the Zealot and <u>Judas the son of James</u>. ¹⁴ All these with one accord were devoting themselves to prayer, together with the women and Mary the mother of Jesus, <u>and his brothers</u>.*

How did his brothers come to believe in their Jesus?

1 Corinthians 15:3 *For I delivered to you as of first importance what I also received: that Christ died for our sins in accordance with the Scriptures, ⁴ that he was buried, that he was raised on the third day in accordance with the Scriptures, ⁵ and that he appeared to Cephas, then to the twelve. ⁶ Then he appeared to more than five hundred brothers at one time, most of whom are still alive, though some have fallen asleep. ⁷ Then he appeared to James, then to all the apostles.*

After Christ was raised from the dead, He made a special appearance to His brother James. Maybe it was through that activity that Judas also became a believer, not a believer during the time of our Lord's earthly ministry, but a believer by the time of the Ascension, and before the day of Pentecost.

Became a servant of Jesus Christ

Jude describes himself in verse 1 as a servant of the Lord Jesus. To be a believer is to be a servant of Christ. If this is the half-brother of Jesus why doesn't he describe himself that way? For that matter, why doesn't James describe himself as Jesus' brother?

- His relationship to Jesus is a **saving** one. Christ began early in the gospels to teach that His brothers and sisters are all those who believe in Him and belong to Him. See the Mark 3 passage quoted above. This is the primary relationship that Jude has with Jesus. Jude understands that, so now when he writes of his relationship to Jesus, he doesn't write of his earthly relationship. His primary relationship to Jesus is now as His servant.
- His relationship to Jesus is a **serving** one. He describes himself as a slave, a δοῦλος (doulos), a bond-servant of Christ. We know from this letter that he was ministering to believers in the church. There is also some indication that he had a ministry in which he was supported.

1 Corinthians 9:1 *Am I not free? Am I not an apostle? Have I not seen Jesus our Lord? Are not you my workmanship in the Lord? ² If to others I am not an apostle, at least I am to you, for you are the seal of my apostleship in the Lord. ³ This is my defense to those who would examine me. ⁴ Do we not have the right to eat and drink? ⁵ Do we not have the right to take along a believing wife, as do the other apostles and the brothers of the Lord and Cephas?*

The conversion of the Lord's own family to faith in Him, AFTER his death and resurrection is a great proof of the reality of the resurrection and the reality of His divine nature.

- His relationship to Jesus is a **serious** one. This letter takes dead aim at dangers to the church, especially false teachers. It contains the most powerful pronouncements of judgment that you'll find anywhere in the New Testament, so we know Judas, the brother of James, as a courageous servant of Christ.

THE AUDIENCE (:2)

We know very few specifics concerning either the time or destination of this letter. The best guess is somewhere in the 60's AD, somewhere close to the writing of 2 Peter. We don't know whether Jude was written before or after

2 Peter, but they were probably written around the same time. It appears that Jude wrote with specific dangers in mind. That would argue for a specific location for letter, but that location isn't identified. Some say this is a "catholic" (universal) letter, intended for anyone who might read it.

What we do know is that the readers are facing SERIOUS dangers that concern Jude greatly. He must address specific issues. He's writing to protect them, and he is also calling upon them to protect this message. You see that in verse 3: *Beloved, although I was very eager to write to you about our common salvation, I found it necessary to write appealing to you to <u>contend for the faith</u> that was once for all delivered to the saints.* Verse 4 tells us why: *For certain people have crept in unnoticed....*

There's something going on that threatens the purity of the teaching of the gospel, so he's calling them to SERIOUS action. In fact, he's so concerned about what's going on that he can't even write about what he wants to write about. There's an issue that he must address. Jude is urging them to <u>contend</u> for the faith. We'll look at his exhortations. But first, notice his words of assurance. He begins and ends his letter with encouragement.

They are in the midst of a stormy sea of serious danger, and the winds are blowing, and the letter is shouting for a call to arms, and yet at the beginning of this letter and at the end of this letter, there is set for us the proper mindset for such a battle.

If you go to battle for the gospel, don't do it in a spirit of fear. Do it in a spirit of faith. Yes, there's a fight to be engaged in. But you must engage in that battle understanding that you have nothing to fear, because the sovereign God has saved you. He's called you. He loves you, and He will keep you. He doesn't just intend to keep you. He has the power to keep you. As verse 24 says, He *is able.* Those who are to engage in this fight are those who are most secure because of the sovereign, saving work of our God. Jude encourages them by telling them who they are.

The Called

As you know, the New Testament talks about more than one kind of calling.

<u>General call</u>—This is the preaching of the gospel.

Matthew 22:14 *For many are called, but few are chosen.*

Jesus speaks of His own choice in Matthew 11:27, and then issues a general call in the very next verses.

Matthew 11:27 *All things have been handed over to me by my Father, and no one knows the Son except the Father, and no one knows the Father except the Son and anyone to whom the Son chooses to reveal him. 28 Come to me, all who labor and are heavy laden, and I will give you rest. 29 Take my yoke upon you, and learn from me, for I am gentle and lowly in heart, and you will find rest for your souls. 30 For my yoke is easy, and my burden is light.*

This general call can be resisted. It <u>is</u> resisted by many. Jesus acknowledged that.

Luke 13:34 *O Jerusalem, Jerusalem, the city that kills the prophets and stones those who are sent to it! How often would I have gathered your children together as a hen gathers her brood under her wings, and you would not!*

<u>Effectual call</u>—This call effects (produces) something. It is internal. It is not issued to everyone, only to the elect of God. It always results in salvation. All who receive this calling repent and believe. This is why *CALLED* is used to describe those who have believed. We have been called through the general call; we heard the gospel. But we've also been called internally. We received a supernatural call from God that brought us to Jesus, resulting in repentance and faith.

1 Corinthians 1:22 *For Jews demand signs and Greeks seek wisdom, 23 but we preach Christ crucified, a stumbling block to Jews and folly to Gentiles, 24 but to those who are called, both Jews and Greeks, Christ the power of God and the wisdom of God.*

Some hear Christ preached as God's power and God's wisdom. This call was not in their ears, but in their hearts. Paul wrote the book of Romans *To all those in Rome who are loved by God and called to be saints.* (Romans 1:7).

Romans 8:30 *And those whom he predestined he also called, and those whom he called he also justified, and those whom he justified he also glorified.*

If you were predestined for salvation, eventually you were called. And if you were called, you were justified; saved. And you will be glorified. In fact, in the language of Romans 8:30, you have already been glorified. God sees it as finished. From eternity past to eternity future there's this unbroken chain of redemption, and God is the one who has brought it to pass.

Beloved

This is in the perfect tense, indicating something that has existed in the past and has continuing results. God placed His love on believers in eternity past with results that continue in the present and into the future.

Ephesians 1:3 *Blessed be the God and Father of our Lord Jesus Christ, who has blessed us in Christ with every spiritual blessing in the heavenly places, ⁴ even as he chose us in him before the foundation of the world, that we should be holy and blameless before him. In love ⁵ he predestined us for adoption through Jesus Christ, according to the purpose of his will, ⁶ to the praise of his glorious grace, with which he has blessed us in the Beloved.*

How do you explain our calling? Only by God's gracious love.

Kept by Jesus Christ

His readers—and we—are *kept by Jesus Christ* or as ESV and others put it, *kept for Jesus Christ*. The meaning is that we are kept by Jesus Christ, by His power, or that we are kept for the day of Christ, until we're revealed with Him. Both are true. Either way, we are God's people, kept by God, guarded in the faith. Each of these verbs is in the passive voice. These things were done not by us, but to us.

- **God called us.**
- **God loved us.**
- **Christ keeps us.**

When we are under assault, we can walk through this in a very practical way.

1. Why am I a believer? God called me.
2. Why did God call me? God loved me.
3. What could separate me from this love? Nothing! He will keep me.

God has the power to do this (:24-25). Yet this doesn't rule out our responsibility. We must persevere (:21). God will keep you, and He will do it while producing in you the desire and the ability to walk with Christ.

THE AIM (:2)

Even though it's a letter full of truth about a spiritual battle, Jude wants certain blessings for his readers:

- **Multiplied mercy**—God's pity and grace towards us. Jude wants us to experience God's compassion in its fullness.
- **Multiplied peace**—The peace that comes from God. Jude wants God's peace to be continuing and increasing in our lives.
- **Multiplied love**—A knowledge of His love for us and the expression of His love through us. Jude wants God's love to flourish in and among and through us.

APPLYING IT

Let's remember three things from these verses:

1. <u>We can have confidence about believers in times of turmoil</u>. God called them. God loves them God will keep them, and He is able to keep them from stumbling. God finishes what he starts.

Philippians 1:6 *And I am sure of this, that he who began a good work in you will bring it to completion at the day of Jesus Christ.*

2 Thessalonians 3:4 *And we have confidence in the Lord about you, that you are doing and will do the things that we command.*

2. <u>Human effort is still required</u>. If you see ANYTHING in Paul's letters about his concern for the churches, and in this letter of Jude's as well, it is that believers can be in serious danger, and that they must engage in the conflict in accordance with God's word.

3. <u>We can know calm within us while a storm rages around us</u>. Jude is writing to people who are in the midst of turmoil, yet he prays that mercy, peace and love be multiplied to them.

9
CHANGE OF PLANS
(Jude 3-4)

This power-packed little letter from the pen of Jude is the only one we have from him. It describes a change in plans. It's not the letter he originally intended to write. It is the best "plan B" you will ever encounter. God inspired it and intended it to be in the canon of scripture. Jude tells us he was hurrying, intending to write a letter about the salvation that they all have in common. He doesn't tell us exactly what he was going to write about, but from his description, it would have been a letter with a different tone from this one. Maybe he intended to write a letter of encouragement and family rejoicing, celebrating our salvation. While he was eagerly making the effort to write, he was, literally, *compressed*, feeling a sense of necessity laid upon him to head in a different direction. Instead of the tone of a family celebration, this letter has the tone of an army being called to take up arms. Something that you see both in the apostles, and here in Jude, is that these men who served the church in the earliest days were sensitive to the direction of the Holy Spirit. Look at the actions of the apostle Paul and Timothy:

Acts 16:6 *And they went through the region of Phrygia and Galatia, having been forbidden by the Holy Spirit to speak the word in Asia. ⁷And when they had come up to Mysia, they attempted to go into Bithynia, but the Spirit of Jesus did not allow them. ⁸So, passing by Mysia, they went down to Troas. ⁹And a vision appeared to Paul in the night: a man of Macedonia was standing there, urging him and saying, "Come over to Macedonia and help us." ¹⁰And when Paul had seen the vision, immediately we* *sought to go on into Macedonia, concluding that God had called us to preach the gospel to them.*

In our last chapter, we looked at the first two verses, noting that Jude's readers are *called.* That call imparts a responsibility. In verses 3-4, we are told why he was redirected, what God used to place this necessity upon him, and what responsibility God has delivered to us. That is found in the words *contend earnestly for the faith.* Verses 3 and 4 show us the responsibility this phrase imparts and what contending for the faith involves.

THE ATTITUDE FOR CONTENDING FOR THE FAITH

Along with this responsibility, Jude gives us an example. The motivation of a proper kind of contending for the faith is a love for God's people. This includes those in the present and also those who will become believers in the future.

Love for God's people

When we think of contending for the faith, love is probably not one of the first things to come to our minds. But Jude begins this section with the word *Beloved.* Jude loves these people. We contend for the faith because of the glory of God, but also for the good of God's people. We must contend for the purity of the gospel for the sake of souls. At the forefront of Jude's mind is the fact that these people are loved by God.

Understanding who they are—They are the *called,* the *loved.* and the *kept,* mentioned verse 2. These people are the objects of God's eternal plan of salvation, loved by Him from all eternity.

Understanding who they are to God—In Acts 20, Paul meets with the Ephesian elders. He instructs them to contend for the faith on behalf of the church because it is precious to God, purchased by Christ's own blood.

Acts 20:28 *Pay careful attention to yourselves and to all the flock, in which the Holy Spirit has made you overseers, to care for the church of God, which he obtained with his own blood.? 29I know that after my departure fierce wolves will come in among you, not sparing the flock; 30and from among your own selves will arise men speaking twisted things, to draw away the disciples after them. 31 Therefore, be alert, remembering that for three years I did not cease night or day to admonish every one with tears. 32And now I commend you to God and to the word of his grace, which is able to build you up and to give you the inheritance among all those who are sanctified,*

Understanding how they are to be cared for—God's people are cared for with the truth of God's word. Sound doctrine includes both pure teaching and pure living. Satan seeks to infiltrate the church. He wants the church to adopt impure teaching and impure living. The Bible counteracts both of those, so the devil tries to attack the Bible or to sideline it or to undermine it. The Bible is our offensive weapon against his schemes. The church must be guarded on the battlefront of doctrine. The defense takes place at the point of the truth.

We contend for the faith because we love God and we love His people.

Necessity because of God's truth

The second attitude you see in Jude is a sense of urgency concerning the church's health and well-being. When he says in verse 3, *I was very eager to write to you*, the NASB has *I was making every effort to write you*. That is, he was actively trying to write this letter, but something changed his course. He shows a sense of duty, urgency and constraint regarding *the faith*. This is the whole body of objective truth, the gospel in the fullest sense. It was *delivered* to us—handed over to us, passed down to us, or given into our care. We have received a deposit of truth for which we are now responsible. It was deposited *once for all time.* ἅπαξ (hapax) is the Greek word that speaks of something that has been accomplished and won't be repeated. Several attitudes are conveyed through these words:

- A recognition of a once-delivered body of truth that is to be contended for. We have the Bible. It's now complete.
- A recognition of the importance of not allowing that message to be distorted to the destruction of souls. Do we take the Word of God seriously?
- The courage necessary to defend that body of truth. He's not allowing tolerance of false doctrine. He's calling for conviction. A strong conviction about the Word of God is not only allowed. It's required.
- The desire to rejoice and celebrate as much as the desire to contend. Some people know only a contender's spirit. That's not the spirit for this work. Jude intended to write to them about their common salvation, but he felt compelled to change the subject. Having said that, we can't be cowards. When a fight is necessary, we must be willing to take up the battle for the faith. We are to contend for the faith, but are not to be, as a pattern, contentious people. Nor are we to suspect everyone of being an enemy of the

gospel, nor attack the friends of the gospel. Contending was not Jude's delight. It was his duty.

Confidence in God's power

We know the security of God's people (:1-2). Although we need to engage in these skirmishes, we can be confident that the ultimate end has been settled.

We know the faithfulness of God's dealings (:24-25). He will preserve us until the very end.

We know the importance of God's chosen means (:3-23). God will keep His people contending for the faith, so we must not be timid about the responsibility.

THOSE RESPONSIBLE FOR CONTENDING FOR THE FAITH

Ministers - Jude

In writing this letter, Jude is acting as a pastor, a shepherd, an elder. Contending for the faith is especially the work of pastors and elders. In Acts 20 we see the emphasis placed on sound teaching and on contending with those who upset the faith of others. In the pastoral letters, we see this in the examples of the apostle Paul and Jude, and we see that Paul urges Timothy and Titus to watch for souls, to guard the sheep by proclaiming the truth and by insisting on it.[14]

The church as a whole - Those whom he addresses

Besides pastors and elders, he is addressing this to the church at large. He does not say, "Pray for me as I contend for the faith." He urges his readers as a whole to contend for it. We ALL have a responsibility to contend for the faith. We ALL must be ready to address the issue of apostasy and the issue of heresy. Every believer will be exposed to these issues at some time and will be put into the position of defending the truth.

- We will see people walk away from the faith.
- We will be confronted by people bringing their claims of "mysterious truth" to us and wanting us to follow them.

---

[14] 1 Tm 1:3, 18-20; 3:14-16; 4:1-6, 11-16; 5:17-6:21; 2 Tm 2:1-4:5; Titus 1:5-2:1; 2:15-3:11

- We will be asked to give a reason for our hope, for our beliefs.

John MacArthur was on his college track team. His most memorable race was a mile relay that his team lost. Their first runner started wonderfully. He was tied for the lead when he passed the baton to MacArthur, who ran all-out. As he passed the baton to the third runner, they were in the lead. The third runner took the baton and started well. He ran fast about halfway around the track. Then he stopped, walked off the track, and sat down on the grass. MacArthur ran to him, thinking he must have pulled a muscle. MacArthur reached him, and he didn't look like he was in pain. MacArthur asked what was wrong. The reply was, "I don't know—I just didn't feel like running today."[15] The baton of God's Word has been passed down, generation after generation for 2000 years. It is now in our possession. We don't have a right to walk off the track and sit on the grass. We dare not be that third runner. We have been given this deposit of truth, and we are responsible to pass it on to others in purity, willing to contend with error.

THE REASONS FOR CONTENDING FOR THE FAITH

Dangerous people (vs. 4-23)

Their identification

Certain people appear on the scene, sometimes suddenly. We don't know whether Jude received a report of trouble in the churches and that is what prompted this change of course, or whether he was witnessing a pattern of behavior and so felt compelled. Regardless, these people are described in terms of *arising* or *appearing*. Notice that in Acts 20, Paul uses the word *arise*. They have been there all along, unnoticed, but they rise up and are recognized.

Acts 20:30 *and from among your own selves will arise men speaking twisted things, to draw away the disciples after them.*

1. How these people got there—*crept in unnoticed.*

They came in under the guise of being one kind of person, believing one kind of teaching. As they begin to operate in the church, they show their true colors. They try to change the church into their own image. What they want may be something diseased that must be stood against, or it will kill that

---

church. Incidentally, these people may be ordinary church members, or elders, or pastors.

2. Why these people are not a surprise—*who long ago were designated.*

This may mean that these individuals were predestined for this. God certainly knew their destiny before they were born. But it seems that Jude is speaking of the many apostates who have existed throughout redemptive history, and their *condemnation.* Throughout the Old Testament we have examples of apostasy and its judgment. We are told in very plain terms that this will be happening in the church. If you think of church as never having controversy, a place where there are never battles where we must stand up and fight for what's right, you haven't read your New Testament very carefully. There's not a church like that in the Bible. They had the apostles themselves as leaders overseeing the church, but look at Romans, Ephesians, Colossians, Galatians, and the letters to the seven churches in Revelation. Across the board, you find challenges, struggles, things that had to be addressed. Jude says these people *long ago were designated.* That's what Paul tells the Ephesian elders in Acts 20. It's what he tells Timothy.

2 Timothy 4:1 *I charge you in the presence of God and of Christ Jesus, who is to judge the living and the dead, and by his appearing and his kingdom: ² preach the word; be ready in season and out of season; reprove, rebuke, and exhort, with complete patience and teaching. ³ For the time is coming when people will not endure sound teaching, but having itching ears they will accumulate for themselves teachers to suit their own passions, ⁴ and will turn away from listening to the truth and wander off into myths.*

See also 2 Timothy 3:1-9 and 2 Peter 3:1-18.

Their Character

- They are *ungodly.* They live without reference to God, having no fear or reverence for Him. One TV preacher told the story that God was depressed one day and told him to cheer Him up. You see, that man's ungodly statement showed that he had no fear of God. Do you think all people are basically good? You need to re-read your Bible.
- They *pervert grace into sensuality,* using it as an excuse to fulfill the desires of the flesh.
- In this way they *deny...Christ* in their living. Almost none of them come out and say, "I deny Jesus Christ." Instead, they throw off

His lordship, living as their own masters, and using God's grace as the excuse for it.

They do not have a real love for the church, because they are destroying it and tearing it apart.

<u>What these people do</u>

- They <u>cause trouble</u> with their doctrine and lifestyle.
- They <u>disregard authority</u>.
- They <u>operate behind the scenes</u>, scheming and in quiet conversations. They don't operate in a way that's honorable.
- They <u>draw disciples away after themselves</u> by privately passing on their own teachings.

Dangerous Teachings

In this case, they are attacking the gospel by what they teach about grace. You can see hints of their false doctrine throughout this letter, but the emphasis is not on their doctrine. The emphasis is on their living. The gospel can be attacked morally as well as doctrinally. Their false teaching lets them, and others, have lives of sexual immorality and general debauchery in the name of Jesus.

APPLICATION
1. Do we recognize that these things <u>will</u> happen?
2. Do we have the courage to face it? Or will we run? Do we have the heart for it?
3. Can we maintain a godly spirit in it? The church should not be a place of heresy-hunting and judging, where everyone is suspect, except you.

Don't forget that this isn't what Jude set out to do. He had to do it because the circumstances called for it. May the Lord help us to take to our hearts this call to arms and be ready for it!

10
THIS CONDEMNATION
(Jude 5-7)

Jude has told us about dangerous people who have infected the church and who need to be confronted. They came into the church in the name of Christ, professing to be believers. Now both their teaching and their living have made it apparent that they are denying the Lord Jesus Christ. They are marked out for a condemnation prescribed for them long ago.

THE CONDEMNATION IS THAT WHICH BELONGS TO APOSTATES

This condemnation is the judgment that God has pronounced upon those who apostatize from the truth. It was set forth by God long ago, and belongs to anyone, in any age, who is guilty of the sin of apostasy.

These false teachers have come into the church under the guise of belief in the truth, in the name of Jesus Christ, masquerading as believers in the true gospel. They are now doing damage to the church by denying our only Master and Lord through false doctrine and immoral living.

The meaning of apostasy

John MacArthur does a great job of explaining the sin of apostasy.

> It is the abandoning of truth. It is not to be confused with mere indifference to the Word, for it involves an intellectual acceptance of

the Scriptures. Neither is apostasy to be confused with error. It is not necessarily believing false doctrine. An apostate can acknowledge that certain doctrines are true, but fail to believe them in his heart. An apostate can acknowledge Christ without accepting Him... Apostates have received light but not life. They have known and accepted the written Word, but have never met Christ, the living Word... **Apostasy is a deliberate rejection of the truth after it is known.** Hence it is the most damnable sin of all. The writer of Hebrews said, "Of how much sorer punishment, suppose ye, shall he be thought worthy, who hath trodden under foot the Son of God, and hath counted the blood of the covenant, with which he was sanctified, an unholy thing?" (10:29). Somebody who knows the truth and stomps across it deserves more severe punishment than others who didn't know as much. [16]

Scripture warns us repeatedly about this sin.

The warnings concerning apostasy

Here are several scripture passages concerning apostasy:

Colossians 1:21 *And you, who once were alienated and hostile in mind, doing evil deeds, ²² he has now reconciled in his body of flesh by his death, in order to present you holy and blameless and above reproach before him, ²³ if indeed you continue in the faith, stable and steadfast, not shifting from the hope of the gospel that you heard, which has been proclaimed in all creation under heaven, and of which I, Paul, became a minister.*

Verse 23 warns that you are above reproach only if you remain steadfast in the faith.

John 8:31 *So Jesus said to the Jews who had believed in him, "If you abide in my word, you are truly my disciples…"*

The word *abide* means to continue, to remain in His word.

Hebrews 6:1 *Therefore let us leave the elementary doctrine of Christ and go on to maturity, not laying again a foundation of repentance from dead works and of faith toward God, ² and of instruction about washings, the laying on of hands, the resurrection of the dead, and eternal judgment. ³ And this we will do if God permits. ⁴ For it is impossible to restore again to repentance those who have once been enlightened, who have*

---

[16] John MacArthur, "Beware the Pretenders" Sermon

tasted the heavenly gift, and have shared in the Holy Spirit, ⁵ and have tasted the goodness of the word of God and the powers of the age to come, ⁶ if they then fall away, since they are crucifying once again the Son of God to their own harm and holding him up to contempt. ⁷ For land that has drunk the rain that often falls on it, and produces a crop useful to those for whose sake it is cultivated, receives a blessing from God. ⁸ But if it bears thorns and thistles, it is worthless and near to being cursed, and its end is to be burned.

The warning here is for those who have been exposed to the gospel, seen its transforming power in people's lives, yet walk away from it.

1 Timothy 4:1 *Now the Spirit expressly says that in later times some will depart from the faith by devoting themselves to deceitful spirits and teachings of demons…*

The "bottom line" is that unless you continue with Christ, you're not real, no matter what you've said.

The acknowledgement of apostasy

Apostasy is not just a possibility. It's a reality.

1 John 2:19 *They went out from us, but they were not of us; for if they had been of us, they would have continued with us. But they went out, that it might become plain that they all are not of us.*

Mark 4:14 *The sower sows the word. ¹⁵ And these are the ones along the path, where the word is sown: when they hear, Satan immediately comes and takes away the word that is sown in them. ¹⁶ And these are the ones sown on rocky ground: the ones who, when they hear the word, immediately receive it with joy. ¹⁷ And they have no root in themselves, but endure for a while; then, when tribulation or persecution arises on account of the word, immediately they fall away. ¹⁸ And others are the ones sown among thorns. They are those who hear the word, ¹⁹ but the cares of the world and the deceitfulness of riches and the desires for other things enter in and choke the word, and it proves unfruitful. ²⁰ But those that were sown on the good soil are the ones who hear the word and accept it and bear fruit, thirtyfold and sixtyfold and a hundredfold."*

2 Peter 2:20 *For if, after they have escaped the defilements of the world through the knowledge of our Lord and Savior Jesus Christ, they are again entangled in them and overcome, the last state has become worse for them than the first. ²¹ For it would have been better for them never to have known the way of righteousness than after knowing it to turn back from the holy commandment delivered to them. ²² What the true proverb* *says has happened to them: "The dog returns to its own vomit, and the sow, after washing herself, returns to wallow in the mire."*

There are people who will receive the word, but only superficially. They eventually depart from it and return to their former lifestyle.

THE CONDEMNATION CAN BE DEMONSTRATED FROM THE PAST

Jude gives three pictures from the past to illustrate this kind of condemnation. His goal is to remind us that defectors from the truth will always meet with divine judgment.

- Apostate Israelites
- Apostate Angels
- Apostate Gentiles

Apostate Israelites

He uses Old Testament examples they knew well. *"You once fully knew it"* (:5) or, as NASB puts it, *"You know all things once for all"*—Jude is reminding them that they know the gospel and the truth in its fullness, in terms of a faith once delivered. (A side note regarding *"Jesus"*—there is a textual issue here. Some manuscripts have *Jesus*. Others have *Lord*, and could be referring to God the Father, but this doesn't change Jude's main point.[17]) He reminds them that the Exodus was not only a powerful picture of <u>divine love</u>. It was also a powerful picture of <u>divine judgment</u>. This included judgement on the Egyptians, but also on the unbelieving, apostate Israelites. For the most part, the generation that left is not the generation that entered the Promised Land.

Rebellion at Kadesh—God had rescued the Israelites from Egypt and had led them in unmistakable ways. They had come to the brink of entering the Promised Land. When they arrived at Kadesh, all they had to do was believe God and walk in. They sent twelve spies into the land. When they returned, ten said they should not go in. There are big, powerful people there. The

---

[17] For one detailed study of this issue, see
https://www.rts.edu/SharedResources/Documents/Charlotte/student_papers/Midwinter%20Who%20Led%20Israel%20Jude%205.pdf

people didn't believe the two spies, Caleb and Joshua, who said to go ahead. They did not believe God's promises.

Numbers 14:1 *Then all the congregation raised a loud cry, and the people wept that night. ² And all the people of Israel grumbled against Moses and Aaron. The whole congregation said to them, "Would that we had died in the land of Egypt! Or would that we had died in this wilderness! ³ Why is the LORD bringing us into this land, to fall by the sword? Our wives and our little ones will become a prey. Would it not be better for us to go back to Egypt?" ⁴ And they said to one another, "Let us choose a leader and go back to Egypt."*

There's more to the story, but they were judged severely, justly and swiftly, never able to enter the Promised Land. Unbelief led to death and judgment.

Numbers 14:26 *And the LORD spoke to Moses and to Aaron, saying, ²⁷ "How long shall this wicked congregation grumble against me? I have heard the grumblings of the people of Israel, which they grumble against me. ²⁸ Say to them, 'As I live, declares the LORD, what you have said in my hearing I will do to you: ²⁹ your dead bodies shall fall in this wilderness, and of all your number, listed in the census from twenty years old and upward, who have grumbled against me, ³⁰ not one shall come into the land where I swore that I would make you dwell, except Caleb the son of Jephunneh and Joshua the son of Nun. ³¹ But your little ones, who you said would become a prey, I will bring in, and they shall know the land that you have rejected. ³² But as for you, your dead bodies shall fall in this wilderness. ³³ And your children shall be shepherds in the wilderness forty years and shall suffer for your faithlessness, until the last of your dead bodies lies in the wilderness. ³⁴ According to the number of the days in which you spied out the land, forty days, a year for each day, you shall bear your iniquity forty years, and you shall know my displeasure.' ³⁵ I, the LORD, have spoken. Surely this will I do to all this wicked congregation who are gathered together against me: in this wilderness they shall come to a full end, and there they shall die. ³⁶ And the men whom Moses sent to spy out the land, who returned and made all the congregation grumble against him by bringing up a bad report about the land— ³⁷ the men who brought up a bad report of the land—died by plague before the LORD. ³⁸ Of those men who went to spy out the land, only Joshua the son of Nun and Caleb the son of Jephunneh remained alive.*

Apostate angels (:6)

This, again, is a very brief statement. Jude doesn't identify these angels, but assumes they know about them. When you read 2 Peter and look at Jewish tradition outside the scriptures, you find that much was written about these angels. I believe Jude refers to angels that committed the heinous sin that is recorded in Genesis 6:1-4. Some reject the idea that these were angels, because they can't imagine angels cohabitating with women.[18] They say *"sons of God"* refers to the godly line of Seth, and *"daughters of men"* to the women of pagan nations. The problem with that is twofold. First, "sons of God" in the Old Testament refers to angels in three of the four other places where it occurs.[19] Only once does it refer to people, and that exception is very clear.[20] So, when in doubt, we'd expect it to refer to angels.

Second, whatever the sin these angels committed as described in 2 Peter and Jude, it is a reference to an Old Testament occurrence. It's also compared in Jude 7 to the sin of Sodom and Gomorrah, going after *strange flesh*, (KJV and NASB), some kind of unnatural sexual union. In the case of Sodom and Gomorrah, it was homosexuality; in the case of these angels, it seems to have been something sexual. Due to the special judgment that God brought upon them, and the judgment of the flood, this doesn't seem to be a sin that could ever be repeated. Nonetheless, there is overwhelming evidence that this should be understood as a reference to angels. Their sin is described here.

Genesis 6:1 *When man began to multiply on the face of the land and daughters were born to them, 2 the sons of God saw that the daughters of man were attractive. And they took as their wives any they chose. 3 Then the LORD said, "My Spirit shall not abide in man forever, for he is flesh: his days shall be 120 years." 4 The Nephilim were on the earth in those days, and also afterward, when the sons of God came in to the daughters of man and they bore children to them. These were the mighty men who were of old, the men of renown.*

They did not stay within their own position of authority. They went outside the rights that God had assigned to them.

They left their proper dwelling. Heaven was their original and proper dwelling, but these angels descended due to rebellion. They went further, to the point of taking a masculine form and going after *strange flesh*.

2 Peter 2:4 *For if God did not spare angels when they sinned, but cast them into hell and committed them to chains of gloomy darkness to be kept until the judgment; 5 if he did not spare the ancient world, but preserved Noah, a herald of righteousness, with seven others, when he brought a flood upon the world of the ungodly; 6 if by turning the cities of*

---

[18] In the Bible, when angels are seen on earth (not in heaven), their appearance is as adult males.
[19] Job 1:6; 2:1; 38:7
[20] Hosea 1:10

Sodom and Gomorrah to ashes he condemned them to extinction, making them an example of what is going to happen to the ungodly; ⁷ and if he rescued righteous Lot, greatly distressed by the sensual conduct of the wicked ⁸ (for as that righteous man lived among them day after day, he was tormenting his righteous soul over their lawless deeds that he saw and heard); ⁹ then the Lord knows how to rescue the godly from trials, and to keep the unrighteous under punishment until the day of judgment…

Apostate Gentiles (vs.7)

Sodom and Gomorrah serve as an example because they received the punishment of eternal fire, just as the fallen angels have. Jude describes their sin as *sexual immorality* and *unnatural desire*—just as the angels. They knew the truth, because Lot was living among them, yet they walked away. In Genesis 19 we find the account of their sexual immorality, their unnatural desire, and even evidence that Lot was declaring some truth to them.

Genesis 19:1 *The two angels came to Sodom in the evening, and Lot was sitting in the gate of Sodom. When Lot saw them, he rose to meet them and bowed himself with his face to the earth ² and said, "My lords, please turn aside to your servant's house and spend the night and wash your feet. Then you may rise up early and go on your way." They said, "No; we will spend the night in the town square." ³ But he pressed them strongly; so they turned aside to him and entered his house. And he made them a feast and baked unleavened bread, and they ate. ⁴ But before they lay down, the men of the city, the men of Sodom, both young and old, all the people to the last man, surrounded the house. ⁵ And they called to Lot, "Where are the men who came to you tonight? Bring them out to us, that we may know them." ⁶ Lot went out to the men at the entrance, shut the door after him, ⁷ and said, "I beg you, my brothers, do not act so wickedly. ⁸ Behold, I have two daughters who have not known any man. Let me bring them out to you, and do to them as you please. Only do nothing to these men, for they have come under the shelter of my roof." ⁹ But they said, "Stand back!" And they said, "This fellow came to sojourn, and he has become the judge! Now we will deal worse with you than with them." Then they pressed hard against the man Lot, and drew near to break the door down. ¹⁰ But the men reached out their hands and brought Lot into the house with them and shut the door. ¹¹ And they struck with blindness the men who were at the entrance of the house, both small and great, so that they wore themselves out groping for the door.*

Such is the punishment of all those who turn away from the truth.

SUMMARY THOUGHTS
- Apostates are a reality.
- Apostates are recognized when they depart.
- Apostates will be judged with the most severe judgments.

Some of you, even reading a commentary like this, are in a very dangerous position. Some know it. Some don't. All of us must guard against moving away. Think of Psalm 73, which says, *My steps had almost slipped.* How do we guard against moving away? By heeding the warnings in the Scriptures.

APPLICATION
1. Are you real? Is your faith in Christ real? That is, are you saved?
2. If so, will you guard against slippage in your life?
3. If you're not saved, will you repent now? God's Word is sure.
Either way, what will you do with the truth you have been exposed to?

Heed the warning! Never walk away from the truth.

11
DANGER IN THE CHURCH: UNHOLY PEOPLE
(Jude 8-11)

INTRODUCTION

Why are apostates such a big deal? Why does the Bible have stern things to say about them? Jude's description of these people is as stern and severe as anything we could imagine. Are they really that dangerous?

This is a real battle today. We live in a day of unholy tolerance—tolerating sin and error, but not tolerating truth. The spirit of our age makes it difficult to criticize anything except those who, like Jude, stand for truth. The church today struggles: Are there really people, ideas and actions that the Lord would have us stand against? Or would that be unloving, not godly? Though we are to be patient and gentle, in the New Testament you see a very stern approach taken when the church is threatened.

Titus 1:9 [An overseer] *must hold firm to the trustworthy word as taught, so that he may be able to give instruction in sound doctrine and also to rebuke those who contradict it.* ¹⁰ *For there are many who are insubordinate, empty talkers and deceivers, especially those of the circumcision party.* ¹¹ *<u>They must be silenced, since they are upsetting whole families by teaching</u> for shameful gain <u>what they ought not to teach</u>.*

In Jude 8-13 we see in unmistakable terms just how serious it is when you have apostates in the church. The reality of apostates in the church is a serious danger because their presence in the church is an unholy influence. In them, we do not see the building-up work of the Holy Spirit, but the destroying work of the destroyer. Their unholy influence can be recognized under four categories in these verses.

UNHOLY BOLDNESS (:8-9)

Apostates are shameless. They have unholy, insane boldness. In 2 Peter 2:9-16, such people are described as *bold and willful* and are compared to Balaam, *who loved gain from wrongdoing, but was rebuked for his own transgression; a speechless donkey spoke with human voice and restrained the prophet's madness.* He was engaging in madness, and so are these apostates. They're engaging in spiritual insanity; bold because they don't know to be afraid. In these verses, we see that unholy boldness in two ways. It is stated positively and negatively. It is LIKE something and UNLIKE something else.

Boldness like those judged in the past (:8)

The word *yet* is the word μέντοι (mentoi) meaning *yet, however, nevertheless*. Why does Jude use that word? He has just said that the judgment that fell on Sodom and Gomorrah and the surround cities, a punishment of eternal fire, serves as an example. God has given us examples. Jude mentions three: apostate Israel, apostate angels, and apostate Gentiles. In each case, God judged sternly, swiftly, severely, finally. God judges apostates 100% of the time. He *destroyed* those Israelites who came out of Egypt but did not believe. He *has kept in eternal chains under gloomy darkness* the angels who rebelled. Sodom and Gomorrah and the surrounding cities have undergone *a punishment of eternal fire*. These examples in scripture shout out a warning to anyone who would listen. *Yet* right in the face of that example, *these people also* imitate *in like manner* the very people who fell under those judgments. *In like manner* does not necessarily mean that the apostates he's describing are engaging in the same specific sins as the people and the angels he's mentioned. He's saying that despite all those warnings from God, they are engaging in sins that call for God's judgment. They are like someone who'd watch a policeman arrest someone for an offense, and then would promptly commit the same offense right in front of the policeman. Their actions are bold, brazen, unholy, insane. This unholy boldness which invites God's judgment is described in three ways.

The boldness to defile the flesh

What seems to be uppermost in Jude's mind is the unholy boldness to engage in sexual immorality in the name of God. Some modern cults have done this. In the name of God, men take multiple wives, and sometimes child "wives." It's sinful, shameful, and defiling. False religion and sexual immorality go hand in hand. In many cases, the people engaging in it don't even try to cover it up. They do supposedly in the name of God.

The boldness to reject authority
People who have a form of godliness but don't know the power of godliness
are self-willed rebels. Proud and arrogant, exalted in their own minds, they
can no longer be instructed. They despise and reject authority.

Titus 1:9 NASB: *holding fast the faithful word which is in accordance with the
teaching, so that he will be able both to exhort in sound doctrine and to refute those who
contradict.* [10] *For there are many* rebellious men, *empty talkers and deceivers, especially
those of the circumcision,*

Rebellious in that verse (*insubordinate* in ESV) means "not subject to rule." They
won't submit to the lordship of Jesus Christ. This rebellion is expressed both
directly, by throwing off the Word of God, and indirectly in that they won't
submit to church authority. The false sects and cults are often also rebellious
against government in general.

The boldness to blaspheme angels
They imagine that they have the authority to speak railing, self-inflated
judgments against angels. Some think *glorious ones* (δόξα or doxa) doesn't refer
to angels, but when you consider 2 Peter 2 and Jude 9, it's fairly clear that
Jude is referring to angels.

One type of apostate lives in the realm of the unseen world in their
imagination. They imagine that they know things that they're really ignorant
of. They think they have the power and authority to speak against angels,
binding or controlling them. On "Christian" television, you can hear all kinds
of bold pronouncements that supposedly bind Satan and control fallen
angels. People speak of stomping on the devil or beating up the devil or
rebuking the devil.

Boldness unlike holy creatures (:9)
Another way to see this unholy boldness is with a contrast. Jude's point is
that not even Michael the archangel presumed to do what these men do.
There was some dispute about the body of Moses. We wouldn't know
anything about this if not for Jude.

Deuteronomy 34:5 *So Moses the servant of the LORD died there in the land of
Moab, according to the word of the LORD,* [6] *and he buried him in the valley in the land
of Moab opposite Beth-peor; but no one knows the place of his burial to this day.*

Maybe Michael was given the burial detail and had to dispute with Satan
concerning the body. Satan may have claimed a right to it based on some sin

that Moses had committed, but Michael would have insisted that the Lord has redeemed Moses. Or maybe Satan wanted to use Moses' body as a point for idolatry in the life of Israel. Whatever the case, even Michael the archangel did not give a direct rebuke to the devil. Instead, he said, *the Lord rebuke you.* He was careful not to step outside the boundary of his own authority. Notice that Peter ties this issue to the matter of spiritual sense, spiritual knowledge.

2 Peter 2:9 *then the Lord knows how to rescue the godly from trials, and to keep the unrighteous under punishment until the day of judgment, *[10]* and especially those who indulge in the lust of defiling passion and despise authority. Bold and willful, they do not tremble as they blaspheme the glorious ones, *[11]* whereas angels, though greater in might and power, do not pronounce a blasphemous judgment against them before the Lord.*

They should tremble, but they don't have enough sense to tremble. People with true spiritual understanding have the kind of holy restraint seen in Michael.

We should tremble at the disregard for authority that we see in some people who claim to be followers of the Lord Jesus Christ. At best, their disrespect is a sign of extreme spiritual immaturity. At worst, it is a mark of ungodliness. Mature saints are the most mindful of matters of authority. False teachers tend to mock such respect, thinking it needless. Men with bad hearts who imagine themselves mature may roll their eyes and mock a good-hearted brother who is respectful toward authority. Yet the ones without respect are really the ones who need correction.

Boldness birthed out of unholy reliance (:8a)
They did these things because they were *relying on their dreams*. There are two ways we can take that statement.

- They are living from a delusional perspective. They are bold and confident, thinking they're walking in the truth, but they're blind. So, relying on their delusional perspectives, they are emboldened to act like they act.
- They were literally relying on their dreams, saying that they were receiving extra-biblical revelation. They claimed that God had told them to do what they were doing and to believe what they believed.

Both of those kinds of dreamers still exist. Some people live in error and sin, boldly thinking that they're right. Others engage in things like Mormon polygamy, basing it on extra-biblical communication from God.

The New Testament mentions at least **two kinds of apostates.**

1.   Those who would spy out our liberty

Galatians 2:4 *Yet because of false brothers secretly brought in- who slipped in to spy out our freedom that we have in Christ Jesus, so that they might bring us into slavery—*

Legalists rely on the law. Their observance of scripture is very strict but very unspiritual. They pay attention to the letter of it, but they don't have a clue about the spirit of it. They strain at a gnat and swallow a camel.

2 Corinthians 3:5 *Not that we are sufficient in ourselves to claim anything as coming from us, but our sufficiency is from God, who has made us competent to be ministers of a new covenant, not of the letter but of the Spirit. For the letter kills, but the Spirit gives life.*

2.   Those who would pervert our liberty

On the other end of the spectrum, and more in keeping with the people whom Jude had to deal with, are those who turn liberty into license. They turn grace into perversion.

Both kinds are very bold, completely wrong-headed, and <u>deadly</u>.

UNHOLY IGNORANCE (:10)
Jude and 2 Peter both teach us that the root of such behavior is a complete lack of spiritual understanding.

They blaspheme what they do not understand (:10a)
Despite their confident assertions and bold words, they are ignorant about the very things about which they claim to be experts. They claim to deal with the devil, demons and the unseen world, but don't know what they're talking about. John MacArthur wrote, "Their behavior evidenced their incredible ignorance and presumption."[21]

Today, some claim to have been to heaven and back, and are eager to tell us all about it. Yet the apostle Paul, when he was caught up to the third heaven,

---

[21] MacArthur, John Jr., *2 Peter and Jude MacArthur New Testament Commentary* (Chicago: Moody Press, 2005)

was forbidden to tell what he saw. They may be sincere, and some may be Christians, but we don't need their revelations. We have the once-for-all, delivered-unto-the-saints faith (verse 1).

They are destroyed by their instinctive understandings (:10b)
What they DO know, however, is animalistic. They live by their instincts and their senses. These false teachers have instincts about how to get into a church, about how to draw disciples away to themselves, about how to enrich themselves and advance themselves. They are cunning schemers. They think they're getting ahead, but they're on the road that leads to their damnation. They reject truth and authority in order to follow their instincts, and their instincts betray them. If they continue following their instincts, they'll perish. What they think they understand, they don't, and what they do understand is wrong and leads them to destruction.

The church is holy. It is the temple of God. Even when men don't take the church seriously, God takes the church seriously.

1 Corinthians 3:17 *If anyone destroys God's temple, God will destroy him. For God's temple is holy, and you are that temple.*

We've seen that the false teachers are dangerous because of their unholy boldness and their unholy ignorance. Jude mentions a third reason.

UNHOLY AMBITION (:11)
Remember that apostates are not people who lose their salvation. They are people who never had salvation. The apostle John said this of antichrists:

1 John 2:19 *They went out from us, but they were not of us; for if they had been of us, they would have continued with us. But they went out, that it might become plain that they all are not of us.*

What are these men and women after?[22] Because they are not saved, they cannot be motivated by that which motivates true believers and true shepherds. So why are they in the church? From Satan's point of view, they are present because he has sown tares among the wheat. But what's the motivation of these apostates themselves? (Some may be genuinely deceived

---

[22] Apostates or false teachers can be either male or female. The Lord Jesus rebuked the church in Thyatira because they allowed a woman to exert an evil influence she shouldn't have been allowed to exert (Rev. 2:18-29).

and don't know that they are false. If they were to honestly assess their motivations in light of what we see here, they might be rescued.)

Jude describes their motivation by **three comparisons** from the Old Testament. In some way, they are like Cain, like Balaam and like Korah. It's not that every one of them will be totally like all three of those men. Some may be like Cain. Some may be like Korah, others like Balaam. These three men help us understand the apostates' motivation.

Like Cain—with self-styled religion

Cain was the first murderer. What motivated him? The Bible tells us.

1 John 3:12 *We should not be like Cain, who was of the evil one and murdered his brother. And why did he murder him? Because his own deeds were evil and his brother's righteous. 13 Do not be surprised, brothers, that the world hates you. 14 We know that we have passed out of death into life, because we love the brothers. Whoever does not love abides in death. 15 Everyone who hates his brother is a murderer, and you know that no murderer has eternal life abiding in him. 16 By this we know love, that he laid down his life for us, and we ought to lay down our lives for the brothers. 17 But if anyone has the world's goods and sees his brother in need, yet closes his heart against him, how does God's love abide in him?*

Remember from Genesis 4 that Cain and Abel each brought an offering to God. Abel's was acceptable to God, offered in faith. By the way, faith must have an object. God is the object of faith, but faith is acting on information received from God. Faith is not just doing what you think is best. Faith is obeying God, obeying God's Word. These two men probably had some revelation from God, perhaps received through their parents, telling them what God wanted in the way of an offering.

Abel's, a blood offering, was acceptable. Cain's, the work of his own hands, was unacceptable, and he was angry over it. God dealt with him in a very patient, encouraging way. He said, *"If you do well, will you not be accepted? And if you do not do well, sin is crouching at the door. Its desire is for you, but you must rule over it."*

God confronted Cain about what's right and what's unacceptable. He willfully walked in the way that is wrong, and he murdered his brother.

Jude says these men have walked in the way of Cain. What was Cain's way? **Self-styled religion**. He wanted a religion he could control. He resented God's acceptable religion. He hated his brother who worshiped God rightly.

The conflict between these two came down to evil and righteousness. Cain was of the evil one; Abel was of God. Cain's deeds were evil; Abel's deeds were righteous. Cain was hateful in his attitude; Abel was hated.

Anyone who carries malice in their heart toward brothers and sisters in Christ, is in danger of hell. They are giving indications that they don't know Christ at all. One of the chief evidences that we belong in the family of God is that we love one another. But these false teachers have gone the way of Cain. They have known what is right, but they have gone in the way of wrong. It is self-styled. They despise what's right, and they have malice toward those who do what's right.

Like Balaam—with greed and compromise
In his second comparison, Jude compares these apostates to Balaam and says, *for the sake of gain they abandoned themselves to Balaam's error.*

Abandoned themselves translates the word ἐξεχύθησαν (*exechuthēsan*), which conveys a powerful image. It comes from a word that means to pour out, or to gush out, and the idea is that they have poured themselves out in their pursuit of that which characterized Balaam.

Note the different ways that it is translated.

- *Abandoned themselves* (ESV)
- *Ran greedily* (KJV)
- *Rushed headlong* (NASB)
- *Rushed* (NIV)
- *Plunged themselves* (CSB)

A.T. Robertson said, "Ran riotously… 'they were poured out,' vigorous metaphor for excessive indulgence." These men have thrown themselves into sin.

Balaam represents **greed**. His life story is in Numbers 22-24. Balak, king of Moab, sent messengers to Balaam, knowing that he was a seer, knowing that what he prophesied came to pass. He offered Balaam money if he would curse Israel. Balaam, knowing of God's relationship to Israel, nonetheless agreed to go with these people, acknowledging that he couldn't go beyond God's word on the matter, but still willing to attempt it. It was on the way there that the prophet was rebuked by his donkey. This is mentioned in the New Testament in 2 Peter 2:15: *…A speechless donkey spoke with human voice and restrained the prophet's madness.*

But even after trying three times to curse Israel, and three times blessing Israel instead, Balaam gave counsel about how Israel could be harmed.

Balaam represents **compromise with sexual immorality and idolatry**. It was right after Balaam departed from Balak that we read these words:

Numbers 25:1 *While Israel lived in Shittim, the people began to whore with the daughters of Moab. ² These invited the people to the sacrifices of their gods, and the people ate and bowed down to their gods. ³ So Israel yoked himself to Baal of Peor. And the anger of the Lord was kindled against Israel. ⁴ And the Lord said to Moses, "Take all the chiefs of the people and hang them in the sun before the Lord, that the fierce anger of the Lord may turn away from Israel." ⁵ And Moses said to the judges of Israel, "Each of you kill those of his men who have yoked themselves to Baal of Peor."*

⁶ And behold, one of the people of Israel came and brought a Midianite woman to his family, in the sight of Moses and in the sight of the whole congregation of the people of Israel, while they were weeping in the entrance of the tent of meeting. ⁷ When Phinehas the son of Eleazar, son of Aaron the priest, saw it, he rose and left the congregation and took a spear in his hand ⁸ and went after the man of Israel into the chamber and pierced both of them, the man of Israel and the woman through her belly. Thus the plague on the people of Israel was stopped. ⁹ Nevertheless, those who died by the plague were twenty-four thousand.

What was the source of this harlotry and idolatry?

Numbers 31:1 *The Lord spoke to Moses, saying, ² "Avenge the people of Israel on the Midianites. Afterward you shall be gathered to your people." ³ So Moses spoke to the people, saying, "Arm men from among you for the war, that they may go against Midian to execute the Lord's vengeance on Midian. ⁴ You shall send a thousand from each of the tribes of Israel to the war." ⁵ So there were provided, out of the thousands of Israel, a thousand from each tribe, twelve thousand armed for war. ⁶ And Moses sent them to the war, a thousand from each tribe, together with Phinehas the son of Eleazar the priest, with the vessels of the sanctuary and the trumpets for the alarm in his hand. ⁷ They warred against Midian, as the Lord commanded Moses, and killed every male. ⁸ They killed the kings of Midian with the rest of their slain, Evi, Rekem, Zur, Hur, and Reba, the five kings of Midian. And they also killed Balaam the son of Beor with the sword. ⁹ And the people of Israel took captive the women of Midian and their little ones, and they took as plunder all their cattle, their flocks, and all their goods. ¹⁰ All their cities in the places where they lived, and all their encampments, they burned with fire, ¹¹ and took all the spoil and all the plunder, both of man and of beast. ¹² Then they brought the captives and the plunder and the spoil to Moses, and to Eleazar the priest, and to the congregation of the people of Israel, at the camp on the plains of Moab by the*

Jordan at Jericho. ¹³ Moses and Eleazar the priest and all the chiefs of the congregation went to meet them outside the camp. ¹⁴ And Moses was angry with the officers of the army, the commanders of thousands and the commanders of hundreds, who had come from service in the war. ¹⁵ Moses said to them, "Have you let all the women live? ¹⁶ Behold, these, on Balaam's advice, caused the people of Israel to act treacherously against the Lord in the incident of Peor, and so the plague came among the congregation of the Lord."

So, Balaam was killed in battle, fighting against Israel, and he had advised Israel's enemies to have their women lead the Israelites into immorality and idolatry. In the Book of Revelation, Jesus Christ referred to this in his message to the church at Pergamum.

Revelation 2:14 *But I have a few things against you: you have some there who hold the teaching of Balaam, who taught Balak to put a stumbling block before the sons of Israel, so that they might eat food sacrificed to idols and practice sexual immorality. ¹⁵ So also you have some who hold the teaching of the Nicolaitans. ¹⁶ Therefore repent. If not, I will come to you soon and war against them with the sword of my mouth.*

Taken together, the picture is clear. These apostates have run wholeheartedly in the direction that destroyed Balaam. They rush headlong into their desire for money, into their teaching which would lead the people of God into compromise with the world, and specifically into the sins of sexual immorality and idolatry. Their teaching and their example set people free to live in the kind of unholy compromise that leads to destruction.

The church must be vigilant on two fronts—doctrinal and moral. We must recognize the danger of compromise with the culture. The culture is immoral and idolatrous.

Like Korah—with rebellion toward authority and with rebellious ambition
The third comparison is Korah. Jude speaks of those *who perished in Korah's rebellion.* Jude assumes that his readers will know the famous background for each of these comparisons.

Read Numbers 16, which tells that Korah and 250 well-known men of Israel accused Moses and Aaron of going too far. They said everyone in the congregation was holy to God, not just the priests (Aaron and his descendants). They accused Moses and Aaron of exalting themselves above the assembly of the Lord. In verse 11, Moses said, *You've gathered against the Lord.*

The Geneva Bible's notes refer to Korah as "seditious and ambitious."

1.   Korah represents rebellious disregard for authority.

2.   Korah represents rebellious ambition for a place and a role that doesn't belong to him.

Apostates do the same. They engage in *rebellion* (Jude 11). The word is ἀντιλογία (antilogia), meaning "to dispute, to contradict." It is used four times in the New Testament. Jude is thinking of someone who disputes and contradicts and rebels against authority.

In the end, the families of Korah, Dathan and Abiram were swallowed up by an earthquake, and the 250 men were killed by fire that came out from the Lord. Rebellious disregard for authority and rebellious ambition are that serious. Why? Because Israel was holy, and the church is holy. If anyone would destroy the Lord's church, the Lord will destroy them. Apostates are dangerous to the church. They have an **unholy boldness**, an **unholy ignorance**, and an **unholy ambition**. That ambition can include malicious ambition like Cain, greedy ambition like Balaam, and rebellious ambition like Korah.

Woe to them! says Jude. That's a warning, a pronouncement of condemnation. Is your heart right before God? Is your ambition a pure one?

2 Corinthians 5:9 (NASB) *Therefore we also have as our ambition, whether at home or absent, to be pleasing to Him.*

Whether you're at home in the body, or absent from the body (with the Lord), that's to be our one ambition: to please the One who saved us.

APPLICATION

1.   Why did the Lord give us these verses? What are they for us?

   a.   <u>A gracious warning to those in danger of these judgments</u>. You're reading this commentary, but could you be an apostate? Are you a pretender—one who seems to be in the church, but not really in Christ? Hear God's gracious warning through this passage. Repent of your sins and turn to His Son in truth, so you will be saved. Don't continue down the path that leads to death.

b. <u>A gracious warning to those who would be damaged by their influence</u>. Sooner or later, you will meet someone in the church who would lead you down the wrong road. God is calling you to recognize such people and not to allow yourself to be influenced by them.

c. <u>A gracious charge to those who must stand against their influence</u>. We must stand against their influence in the church. God calls us to have the courage to contend for the faith.

2. How do we apply this in our own experience?

a. <u>By being discerning</u>. Yes, false teaching really is as dangerous as Jude says. The false teachers are an unholy influence in the church. They are not doing the **upbuilding** work of the Holy Spirit, but the **destroying** work of the destroyer.

b. <u>By being repentant</u>. Wherever there is sin, there's grave danger. We must each repent of it and pursue Christ with all our heart.

c. <u>By being strong</u>. We must not be influenced by those who will be destroyed.

Our hearts should grieve as we think about those who gather into churches to hear a preacher who just tells imaginative stories or who turns grace into license. Through God's Word, through His Son and through His Spirit we have the truth to protect us from spiritually dangerous people. We must contend for what's true. We must do it with gentleness and patience, yet with urgency and firmness—not because we don't love, but because we do. We must deliver people who are on the way to judgment. We must point them away from falsehood to the truth that is in Jesus Christ, the only Savior.

12
DANGER IN THE CHURCH: UNHOLY PRESENCE
(Jude 12-13)

False teachers are a serious danger to the church. They affect the church through division, dissension, rebellion and impurity. We've seen that they have

- Unholy boldness (vs.8-9)
- Unholy ignorance (vs. 10)
- Unholy ambition (vs. 11) with malice like Cain, greed like Balaam, rebellious sedition and ambition like Korah.

UNHOLY PRESENCE (:12-13)

We can look at verses 12-13 in two ways—what the false teachers are like and what kind of influence they are. We'll look at both. First, their unholy presence in the church is compared to 5 things that happen in nature. That's appropriate, because they are natural people—in Adam, fleshly, unconverted.

They are like...

Hidden Reefs

Some translations have "spots," but the word here is from σπιλάς (spilas) — a ledge of rock. A similar, but different, word from σπῖλος (spilos) is used in 2 Peter 2:12 for *blemishes*. They're hidden reefs. You're sailing in to shore and think you're almost into the safe harbor, but then your ship crashes on a rock formation. The hull splits open and the ship sinks. They're like that—something hidden under the water. You don't see it, but people's lives are ruined as they come in contact with these people, as they are influenced by these people. These people are a hidden force for destruction. You come to the church and think you've come to the place where you're guided into safe harbor. You think the people will influence you for godliness and holiness, but these people ruin those they influence.

Waterless Clouds Swept Along by Winds (compare Luke 11:24-26)

Israel's climate is dry. The rain is necessary for crops. What a disappointment it is when the clouds seem to have rain and then blow away and give nothing. These people are like waterless clouds. They promise much but deliver nothing good. They claim giftedness. They claim to know things. They can be very impressive. But their influence, as we'll see in a moment, is fruitless. And what they claim to know and think they know, they don't really know. And so, they are empty.

Jude may be thinking of **Proverbs 25:14**. "*Like clouds and wind without rain is a man who boasts of a gift he does not give.*" In the case of those Jude is speaking of, they do not give the gift because they don't possess it. They promise what they can't give, like clouds and wind without rain.

Matthew 12:43 says, "*When the unclean spirit has gone out of a person, it passes through waterless places seeking rest, but finds none.*" Demonic spirts are described like beings that are parched and thirsty but can't find anything to quench their thirst. Maybe there's a connection in Jude's mind between the demonic and these waterless clouds. There's nothing there that nourishes, that waters, that really the need.

Fruitless Autumn Trees

Autumn is when farmers and gardeners expect to harvest the year's final crops. This pictures the disappointing reality of a barren harvest. You hope for life-giving fruit to help sustain you through the winter, but there's nothing. There will be hardship in the winter.

Many years ago, there was a man who was on a church staff with me. We served together, and he was a friend. Everything he touched in the ministry died. It didn't matter if it was teaching a Sunday school class or leading an outreach ministry. Everything, everything that he was involved in, in the end, turned out to be fruitless. He was there when I got there, and we served together for nine years. At last, I had to sit down with him—it was one of the hardest things I ever had to do—and tell him, "I just don't believe this is the place of service for you." He got angry. His family left the church. I'm brokenhearted to write that not only did he leave the church, but he returned to a life of sin that he knew before he even claimed to be converted. There was a reason why what he touched was fruitless. He was very legalistic. He seemed to have very high standards, but it was empty. There was nothing there. That's how these men are described.

These trees are doubly dead: dead in the sense of fruitless and dead at the very core. In fact, he describes them as having been uprooted. They are fruitless, and they have no way to produce fruit.

Wild Sea Waves, Casting Up Their Own Shame

The sea kicks its trash up onto the shore for all to see. That's how these people are.

Isaiah 57:20 *"But the wicked are like the tossing sea;*
for it cannot be quiet,
and its waters toss up mire and dirt.
21There is no peace," says my God, "for the wicked."

Jude has told us about these people turning the grace of God into an excuse for immorality and reveling in it unashamed. We'll see more about that in a moment. What they should have been ashamed of was there for people to see. It was like the trash of their life kicking up on the shoreline. Restless. No peace. No sense of stability. No sense of satisfaction.

Wandering Stars

This probably refers to meteors. A "shooting star" flashes brightly onto the scene, and then it's gone. There's no lasting effect, no eternal good.

Their Influence in the Church…

1. **A dangerous presence** – Others will run aground on them. In a lifetime, we usually <u>will</u> meet dangerous people in the church.
2. **A deceptive presence** – They participate in the love feasts, but what they teach and what they live is the antithesis of the love of

Christ. They teach and practice immorality and live for themselves. They pretend to love, but do not fear as they live in hypocrisy.

3. **A selfish presence** (vs.12a) – They are *shepherds feeding themselves*. False shepherds treat the ministry like a job. Their motivation is not love for Christ or love for the people. They are motivated by love for themselves and love for gain. Instead of sacrificing themselves to minister the truth, they view the church as a means by which they enrich themselves and take care of themselves. For true shepherds, the church is not a job. It's a calling. They are motivated not by recompense, but by love for Christ and love for His church. They love the church when they serve a handful of people, and they love it when the Lord chooses to bless them and to give them more responsibility.

4. **A fruitless presence** (vs. 12b) – A faithful worker's fruit may not be visible immediately. William Carey ministered for years on the mission field before God gave one convert. But we look back now at Carey's work and see that God blessed abundantly. When God sends someone, He doesn't send them for no purpose. He blesses what He sends them to do. You may have a ministry like Jeremiah, and you're just to pronounce warnings and judgments, and you don't see many converts. Still, as a true shepherd, God's Word is honored and you're a powerful force for God in that way. But in most cases, God blesses His Word in the planting and the watering and the harvesting, and you see people converted and people grow. Lives are changed. These people, however, are fruitless.

5. **A dead presence** (vs. 12b) – When we're with them, we're in the presence of spiritual death. They're doubly dead, uprooted.

6. **A shameless presence** (vs. 13a) – They are bold-faced in their sinning.

7. **An aimless presence** (vs. 13b) – They're *wandering stars* with no good goal.

8. **A condemned presence** (vs. 13c) – Follow them, and you end up condemned. …*for whom the gloom of utter darkness has been reserved forever.*

How does the Lord rid the church of these people? How does He protect His church from them?

- By **identifying their characteristics.** We're warned, so we can discern who they are.
- By **fortifying the members** of the church against their influence. We're warned, so we don't follow them.

- By **disciplining** those who practice these things. We lovingly warn them and lovingly discipline them. Discipline is one of the ways that the Lord keeps his church pure, healthy and united.

The enemy battles against the church. He takes our work seriously, sowing tares among the wheat. We should, also. The battle we face is not just doctrinal. It's moral. Remember Balaam's error. One of the ways Satan wants to affect the church is through compromise with the world, through immorality. Are we being careful? Are we watching out for the ways that our hearts will be stolen away from Christ? Things you watch on television, things you go to see at the movies, things you listen to in the way of music, places where you go with your friends, things that you engage in with your lifestyle—do you understand that in all of that you and I are to be living holy lives, set apart?

When the Lord saves people, He sets them on a new course. And when the enemy can't get in from a doctrinal door, just watch what he did with Balaam. He's going to try to get in through a different door. And that door has to do with immorality and compromise with the world.

Are you taking that seriously? And I wonder if what we need as a church, what we need individually and together, is to say, "Lord, we need a fresh commitment of our lives to what You saved us for, and to see these things with the seriousness that they deserve, and to see my life for You in the serious light that it ought to be looked at from. Lord, help me to serve You in a fresh way when I see on the pages of Scripture, when I see in the Book of Jude that this is serious."

13
THEIR JUDGMENT FORETOLD
(Jude 14-16)

Jude has given examples of apostasy being judged in the past (:5-7, Israel, angels and Gentiles) and shown the unholy influence of apostates in the present (:8-13, unholy boldness, ignorance, ambition and presence). He now returns to a theme that he introduced in verse 4. These people have been **designated for condemnation.**

He says at the end of verse 13 that for these people "*the gloom of utter darkness has been reserved forever*." The theme of verses 14-16 is the certainty and the cause of the judgment that the Lord will bring upon the ungodly. This is not a parable, myth or legend, but a future reality that is being described so that we would be warned. **What do Jude's warnings proclaim?**

THE CERTAINTY OF THEIR JUDGMENT - *Prophesied long ago (:14)*

Jude quotes here from a book of religious teaching that is not Scripture, not inspired. The book was somewhat popular among the Jews of the time. Today it is known as 1 Enoch. It says almost word for word what Jude 14 and 15 say, though nothing else in Scripture speaks of this prophecy. It appears then, that Jude is quoting 1 Enoch. That does not mean that Jude believed everything in 1 Enoch was true, but that this statement was true.

Since Jude's writing was inspired by the Holy Spirit, we can trust it. Remember that the apostle Paul could quote pagans to make a point.[23]

These verses tell us that from ancient times men have been warned about this judgment. It is only seven generations, including Adam's, into man's existence that he is warned about the end. If this warning were not enough, the flood followed it and gave physical warning.

God doesn't give idle threats. He warns. He warns because He is gracious. His warnings come because it's His nature not to take pleasure in the death of the wicked. If you desire to destroy someone, you don't warn them. You give them no opportunity for remedy. God warns so that people would be delivered from the judgment that is coming, delivered by listening to Him and responding to His call for repentance and faith. Secondarily, by warning, He puts His glory in judgment on display.

THE CAPTAIN OF THEIR JUDGMENT - The Lord will come with angels (:14)

It will be a dramatic and brilliant display of His sovereignty, power and authority. Christ made plain that His judgment will involve the angels.

Matthew 13:36 *Then he left the crowds and went into the house. And his disciples came to him, saying, "Explain to us the parable of the weeds of the field." [37] He answered, "The one who sows the good seed is the Son of Man. [38] The field is the world, and the good seed is the children of the kingdom. The weeds are the sons of the evil one, [39] and the enemy who sowed them is the devil. The harvest is the close of the age, and the reapers are angels. [40] Just as the weeds are gathered and burned with fire, so will it be at the close of the age. [41] The Son of Man will send his angels, and they will gather out of his kingdom all causes of sin and all lawbreakers, [42] and throw them into the fiery furnace. In that place there will be weeping and gnashing of teeth. [43] Then the righteous will shine like the sun in the kingdom of their Father. He who has ears, let him hear.*

The apostle Paul also made plain that Christ's judgment will involve the angels.

2 Thessalonians 1:4 *Therefore we ourselves boast about you in the churches of God for your steadfastness and faith in all your persecutions and in the afflictions that you are*

---

[23] Acts 17:28; 1 Corinthians 15:33; Titus 1:12. See ESV footnotes for the source of each quotation.

enduring. ⁵ This is evidence of the righteous judgment of God, that you may be considered worthy of the kingdom of God, for which you are also suffering— ⁶ since indeed God considers it just to repay with affliction those who afflict you, ⁷ and to grant relief to you who are afflicted as well as to us, when the Lord Jesus is revealed from heaven with his mighty angels ⁸ in flaming fire, inflicting vengeance on those who do not know God and on those who do not obey the gospel of our Lord Jesus.

It will be a <u>personal</u> judgment - they will face him whom they have mistreated. (:15)

When he says, *"against Him,"* it doesn't mean only things spoken directly against the Lord Jesus Christ, but it also refers to things spoken against the church. For example, think of what the Lord Jesus said to Paul on the way to Damascus.

Acts 22:7 *"And I fell to the ground and heard a voice saying to me, 'Saul, Saul, why are you persecuting me?'"*

Although Jesus wasn't on the earth when Saul was carrying out his persecution, it was done to His people. Persecuting them is to persecute Christ. One day, all those who have sinned against the Lord Jesus are going to look into the face of the One whom they have blasphemed and rejected, as He judges them.

It will be a <u>powerful and dramatic</u> judgment - the angels will participate and powerfully gather sinners together for their judgment.

The words used to describe the scene speak of its power and majesty.

> 1.   Jesus directs the scene – *"the son of man will send his angels"* (Matthew 13:41)
> 2.   The angels appear with the glorious one – *"holy ones"* (Jude 14)
> 3.   The angels execute his command – *"they will gather out of his kingdom... and throw them into the fiery furnace"* (Matthew 13:41-42)
> 4.   The judgment will be terrible and terrifying – *"fiery furnace, … weeping and gnashing of teeth"* (Matthew13:42); *"flaming fire, inflicting vengeance"* (2 Thess. 1:8)
> 5.   The judgment will be a vindication of all that is right

Matt.13:43 *"Then the righteous will shine like the sun in the kingdom of their Father. He who has ears, let him hear."*

That which is sinful will be exposed as sinful, and that which is righteous will be held forth as righteous.

2 Thess. 2:8 *"...in flaming fire, inflicting vengeance on those who do not know God and on those who do not obey the gospel of our Lord Jesus."*

We should not speak of God's future judgment on sinners without recognizing it was what we deserved by nature. God has had mercy upon us. He's forgiven us, saved us and given all these warnings.

God warns because He is gracious, so that we should sound His warnings. Our attitude should not be harsh, but compassionate. We should say, "God's judgment is coming, and O, that you would flee from it, that you would escape it! Come to Christ and be saved. Come to Christ and have your sins washed away. Come to Christ and be reconciled to God." **That** is our message.

It will be a _promised_ judgment - to _execute_ judgment.

This has been promised in advance. The sentence has already been passed; the guilty are awaiting its execution, yet there is still opportunity to be delivered from it. You must repent of your sins, placing your faith in His Son, from your heart. God is willing to reconcile you to Himself on those terms.

John 3:18 *Whoever believes in him is not condemned, but whoever does not believe is condemned already, because he has not believed in the name of the only Son of God.*

It will be a _particular_ judgment.

The Lord will reprove the lost in specific ways for what they have done. They will be confronted with their sins, their deeds and their words, and they will be **convinced** of their guilt. The word *convict* here means to convince, to make plain, to bring to light. On that day, sins will be exposed in plain light so that men will see what they've done.

An example of this is seen in Matthew 25:31-46.

- Separation of sheep and goats—your individual condition is known by God.
- Those blessed—humble in their service to the Lord.
- Those cursed—unaware of their sin in the light of what true sin is,

condemned to eternal punishment. The story of the Pharisee and tax collector in Luke 18 is also an example of this.

THE CONVICTIONS IN THEIR JUDGMENT

What people and what actions and what sins will be exposed as evil?

All ungodly people - All of lost humanity.

This final judgment takes place in phases, but the final phase is seen in the book of Revelation at the Great White Throne.

- It begins with judgments poured out in the tribulation period
- It continues in the judgment of the nations at the end of the tribulation
- There is a judgment that follows Satan's final rebellion at the end of the millennial kingdom
- There is the Great White Throne judgment.

Read Revelation 20.

All ungodly deeds - Judged for their works

All ungodly ways - Judged for their motives and ambitions and practices

All ungodly speech - Judged for their words.

The thread that runs through it all is the word *ungodly*. It refers to anyone who does not have a proper reverence for God at the core of their life. In contrast, a believer believes, loves the Lord, worships, bows, and gives Him the respect He is due. This is possible only because God mercifully accepts it from those who are in Christ and clothed in grace.

THE CHARACTER OF THOSE JUDGED - Known by their mouths

Grumblers—(γογγυσταί, gongystai)—This is the only place in the New Testament where this Greek noun is used, but it's used in the Septuagint to describe Israel's murmurings against God. (Exodus 16:7-9; Numbers 14:27, 29). A related word is in John 6:41 and 1 Corinthians 10:10.

Complainers— ESV has *malcontents*. The word μεμψίμοιροι (mempsimoiroi) comes from "to blame" plus the word for "allotment." It describes one who is perpetually discontent and dissatisfied, finding fault with God, His plan and purpose.

Lust finders - They are self-willed, led by their flesh, living their lives in pursuit of their own desires.

Boasters – "*Great swelling words,*" not only about themselves, but in the religious sense as well. Their words may be grand and eloquent, with the appearance of wisdom and much learning, but empty of true spiritual food. For example, read this excerpt from a sermon delivered during Easter week.

> As we journey through this Holy Week together, we will hear story after story of retreats to the basic, the animal, the fearful, the reptilian that is still in us all. We will remind ourselves of the great evil that can proceed from this good evolutionary adaptation when it is allowed to go unchecked by grace. It will not be easy. It will feel too familiar. We will be reminded how mightily difficult it can be to stay human, to be like unto God, in a world full of threats both real and perceived. But in the end, we will also be reminded of the good, good news that we are not finally reptilian, we are not finally trapped in our evolutionary heritage, that there is one powerful beyond measure nearby whispering, 'Do not fear, put away your sword, I forgive you, you are mine. '[24]

These impressive words are utter nonsense. The man who preached this sermon is exactly the kind of man that Jude writes about here, unless the Lord Jesus has mercy on him and saves him.

---

[24] Old South Church, March 16, 2008, page 5 from www.oldsouth.org/sermons/qgc16mar08.htm . The sermon is no longer available at that site. The sermon was delivered at a church that had been founded by Puritans in 1669.

Schemers - Telling people what they wanted to hear to advance themselves. They were manipulators.

Korah's rebellion against Moses, found in Numbers 16, tells that via speech, he exerted a major influence in the congregation resulting in the deaths of 14,700 people. He had his 250 men of renown who joined him in death. Read Numbers 16:41-50 to discover the shocking response from those who were spared death in the incident.

The Book of Jude tells us that these people who will be judged one day by the Lord Jesus have mastered the art of showing favoritism to gain advantage.

When thinking about a world facing judgment, look at it with a broken heart, but long for the day when God's name and cause will be vindicated. Don't forget that God has warned about this from the beginning, so heed His warnings and warn people to flee from the wrath that's coming. Those who don't know Jesus need to know that God gives warnings because He desires their salvation. They need to know that He is willing to forgive, on His terms. We yearn for them to turn from their sins and trust in His dear Son for life.

14

THE BELIEVER'S RESPONSE TO APOSTASY

(Jude 17-23)

Jude now turns our attention to what our response should be to apostasy and those who promote it. His habit is to deal in threes. Here, he points out three things we must be concerned with as we address the problem: how we are to regard the apostates (:17-19), how we are to regard ourselves (:20-21) and how we are to regard others (:22-23).

HOW WE REGARD THE APOSTATES (:17-19)

It's important for us to know how to think about apostates.

Apostates are not a surprise

Apostates were predicted by the apostles. End-time prophecies were being fulfilled during Jude's lifetime, and they are being fulfilled in ours. Jude urges us to *remember*. That means more than just calling to mind. It includes allowing the words to make an imprint on your life. The apostles warned about apostates. Here is one such warning.

Acts 20:28 *Pay careful attention to yourselves and to all the flock, in which the Holy Spirit has made you overseers, to care for the church of God, which he obtained with his own blood. ²⁹ I know that after my departure fierce wolves will come in among you, not sparing the flock; ³⁰ and from among your own selves will arise men speaking twisted things,* *to draw away the disciples after them. ³¹ Therefore be alert, remembering that for three years I did not cease night or day to admonish everyone with tears.*

Apostates are a sign of the times

God's people were warned specifically about *scoffers* (in this case those who scoff at the law of God) who follow *their ungodly desires*, reflecting their lack of respect for the Lord. The presence of these scoffers would characterize the *last days*. The *last days* began with the first advent of Christ and will end with the second advent of Christ. The things that characterize the last days in general will probably intensify just prior to His return.

2 Timothy 3:1 *But understand this, that in the last days there will come times of difficulty. ² For people will be lovers of self, lovers of money, proud, arrogant, abusive, disobedient to their parents, ungrateful, unholy, ³ heartless, unappeasable, slanderous, without self-control, brutal, not loving good, ⁴ treacherous, reckless, swollen with conceit, lovers of pleasure rather than lovers of God, ⁵ having the appearance of godliness, but denying its power. Avoid such people.*

Apostates are known by their conduct

They are divisive. They *cause divisions*. The idea is that they *make distinctions*. They separate some out from the rest to "instruct them." Those who follow their teachings are considered "spiritual," and those who don't, are not. They have no fear of the Lord, no fear of dividing His church, no fear of wreaking havoc and damage in the church. They're more concerned with advancing themselves and their agenda than about the unity of the church.

They are worldly. The word is ψυχικός (psuchikos), soulish or natural, as to the lower nature. The King James translates it as *sensual*. They are characterized by ungodly passion. The ones who are truly unspiritual, are those causing the divisions, picking out the weak and the unstable, drawing them away as personal disciples. When there are problems in the church that cause irreconcilable and irreparable divisions, many times it is an issue of salvation.

Acts 20:30 *and from among your own selves will arise men speaking twisted things, to draw away the disciples after them.*

In Ephesians, we learn that they feast on the immature, not being motivated in a holy direction.

Ephesians 4:14 *so that we may no longer be children, tossed to and fro by the waves and carried about by every wind of doctrine, by human cunning, by craftiness in deceitful schemes.*

They do not have the Holy Spirit. They are *devoid of the Spirit*, or literally *not having the Spirit*. This is why they are not motivated in a holy direction and are characterized by ungodly passion, following after worldly lusts. Since they don't have the Holy Spirit, they don't have the holy ambitions and desires He teaches and produces. Remember that in the church, **a seemingly disobedient believer may not really be a believer at all and may not have the Holy Spirit.**

In summary, this is how we think about the apostates. They do not surprise us when they appear. We realize that we will have these battles in the last days, and we recognize what we are dealing with when we deal with them. We are dealing with people who are not bothered by dividing the church, who are natural instead of spiritual, and they are natural because they don't have the Holy Spirit.

HOW WE REGARD OURSELVES (:20-21)

What God wants from us, however, is not only that we would be alert and focus on those who cause trouble in the church. He also wants us to focus on our own walk with Him.

Tom Schreiner has commented, "Love for God cannot thrive when believers devote all their attention to the deficiencies of others." If all we do is focus on the deficiencies of others, we put ourselves in spiritual harm's way. If we are not careful, we can lose sight of our own condition and our own walk with God. Here in verses 20 and 21, we're told not to do that.

The Greek has only one imperative, *keep* (:21), plus three instrumental participles. Given Jude's use of triads in this book, we should probably interpret this as giving us three ways that we *keep* ourselves *in the love of God*. We can then be fortified against the apostates and not fall prey to them. The New American Standard brings this out:

Jude 1:20 *But you, beloved, building yourselves up on your most holy faith, praying in the Holy Spirit, ²¹ keep yourselves in the love of God, waiting anxiously for the mercy of our Lord Jesus Christ to eternal life.*

The Command—Keep yourselves in the love of God

While God keeps you, at the same time He's at work fueling your perseverance. There are two ways to understand what he means by *keep yourselves in the love of God.*

- Maintain your love FOR God, an objective genitive.
- Keep yourself in the place where you experience God's love, a subjective genitive. That would be the place of obedience and submission in the midst of the struggle.

Both are necessary. We cannot maintain love for God unless we keep ourselves in the place where we are aware of and experiencing His love for us. In other words, we must love God, and we love God as we keep ourselves in a place of submission and reverence before Him.

The Conditions

Keeping ourselves in the love of God is active. God keeps us, but we are not passive.

We must be growing. We must commit ourselves to spiritual growth. How? By *building* our lives in our *most holy faith.* This is not just believing more strongly. It's building ourselves up in the faith, the body of faith, that he says we're to contend for. We grow in the Christian life as we learn, believe and practice the Word of God. We don't grow simply by sitting under the teaching of the Word of God, or because we hear it or because we write notes about it. Many people struggle in their walk with God, not because they don't **know** the answers that scripture gives, but because **they won't practice them.**

We must be praying. Jude isn't talking about a mere form of prayer. He is talking about REAL prayer, prayer that reflects the fact that the Holy Spirit is present in our lives. We need prayer that reflects the Holy Spirit's truth, His power, His earnestness, and His help.

We must be waiting. We must be waiting for Christ to return—waiting with anticipation and desire. Waiting with humility, knowing that we need mercy. Waiting with faith, knowing that mercy will be present and that eternal life will be the outcome. You cannot do this if you immerse yourself in the world and live as if Christ is not coming again.

HOW WE REGARD OTHERS (:22-23)

Mercy for some—Those who are struggling with doubts and confusion. They are those affected by the false teachers, but least affected by them.

Forceful rescue for some—Those who are in danger of being taken captive. They are more affected by the false teachers.

Cautious rescue for some—Those who have already been defiled by the false teaching. They are the ones most affected. To them, we show fear and hatred: hatred for the error; fear of the power and influence of the error. Yet we show mercy by doing anything we can take to rescue them.

Jude uses very graphic language to describe the danger present with the group most affected. The word for *garment* referred to clothing worn under the outer garments, next to the skin. The word for *stain* is the word for excrement. Just as you wouldn't want to handle someone's dirty underwear that had been soiled, so you must see that those who have been poisoned spiritually have filth on them, so that even while you seek to help them, you don't allow yourself to be soiled in the process.

Schreiner — "Believers are to beware lest their mercy is transposed into acceptance, and they themselves become defiled by the sin of those they are trying to help."[25]

Mercy, in this case, is probably displayed mostly through prayer.

---

[25] Schreiner, Thomas R., *1, 2 Peter, Jude: An Exegetical and Theological Exposition of Holy Scripture* (Nashville: B&H Publishing Group, 2003), p. 489

15
DOXOLOGY
(Jude 24-25)

These are days of apostasy, but they are by no means the first challenges the church has faced. From the very beginning, the church has faced attacks from without and apostasy from within. We've seen that Jude wrote his book because of what he was witnessing in his own day. He wanted to write about what we share in salvation but felt compelled by God to write to His people, urging them to contend for the faith that was delivered unto the saints once for all.

The book of Jude is a call to arms. It's a call to alertness, a call to readiness, and a call to defend the truth. Yet he ends it the way that he began it. He is positive and celebratory with confidence in the Lord's work in the readers. In the beginning, he identified his readers as those who are kept for Jesus Christ. At the end, he finishes with a doxology, praising God for the fact that His people will not succumb to apostasy. Our confidence in days of apostasy is not found in our strength, our wisdom or our resolve. Our confidence is found in God's power and faithfulness!

THE ONE WORTHY OF THIS PRAISE

God is the one who is worthy and able to keep and to make us stand before His own presence.

He is able to keep (guard) us.

He keeps us in such a way that we don't stumble. Preservation cannot be separated from perseverance. The scriptures clearly teach the eternal security of the Christian. We have done nothing to deserve salvation— therefore, we can do nothing to lose it. Too often people have talked about "eternal security" without understanding that what they are really rejoicing in, is the doctrine of **perseverance**. You are not saved simply because you asked Jesus into your heart and live any way you wish. That is a wrong view of perseverance. Those who will be saved are those who <u>continue</u> in the faith, and the <u>reason</u> they continue is that God has given them a faith that will not fail. He keeps them in faith until the end.

Revelation 14:12 *Here is the perseverance of the saints who keep the commandments of God and their faith in Jesus.* (NASB)[26]

When God is described as the One *who is able to keep* us *from stumbling*, it means He is the One who is able to keep us in the truth and keep us in our faith in Christ. The book of James says *we all stumble in many ways* (James 3:2), meaning that we all still sin, but that's not how Jude is using *stumbling*. Jude doesn't mean that He keeps us from sinning. He is using the word *stumble* as it's used in 2 Peter, where the idea is to fall or fail.

2 Peter 1:10 *Therefore, brothers, be all the more diligent to confirm your calling and election, for if you practice these qualities you will never fall.*

Despite our weakness, God is able to keep people like us from falling away from Jesus. We must praise Him, because He keeps us all the way to heaven.

1 Peter 1:3 *Blessed be the God and Father of our Lord Jesus Christ! According to his great mercy, he has caused us to be born again to a living hope through the resurrection of Jesus Christ from the dead, to an inheritance that is imperishable, undefiled, and unfading, kept in heaven for you, who by God's power are being guarded through faith for a salvation ready to be revealed in the last time.*

---

[26] In this verse, NIV, NLT, ESV, and CSB translate the word Ὧδε (Hode) as *this calls for* or something similar, thus making the verse a **call** to perseverance instead of an **example** of perseverance. It seems better and simpler to follow KJV, ASV, NKJV, NASB, WEB and many commentaries in translating it as *here is*.

<u>Salvation</u> is a settled reality. It's final. And there's another settled reality: anyone who really possesses salvation also experiences a <u>sanctifying</u> reality in their life. Saints will produce differing amounts of fruit—some 30, some 60, some 100-fold. Not every saint reaches the same kind of maturity or proves to be as productive as they should be. But everyone who has been given genuine saving faith in Christ has a that faith will not fail. He guards us from stumbling into the very sins described in this book, that is, into apostasy.

1 Peter 5:10 *And after you have suffered a little while, the God of all grace, who has called you to his eternal glory in Christ, will himself restore, confirm, strengthen, and establish you.*

He is able to make us stand in his glory.

God has the power to keep us from stumbling and falling away, and the verse also says He has the power and ability to *present* us, literally, to *make* us *stand blameless*, before the presence of His glory with great joy. We <u>now</u> stand in grace (Romans 5: 1-4), and we <u>will</u> stand in glory (Colossians 3:4; 1 Peter 5:10).

Colossians 3:4 *When Christ who is your life appears, then you also will appear with him in glory.*

<u>Fallen, Undone Before God</u>

This can only be appreciated when we remember what it means for fallen man to stand in the presence of God's glory. On earth, the consistent picture has been one of terror and dread. The following examples remind us that the closer we are to the Lord, the clearer our vision becomes. We become more aware of our own sinfulness and of God's power and glory.

Isaiah became aware of his unclean lips.

Isaiah 6:5 *And I said: "Woe is me! For I am lost; for I am a man of unclean lips, and I dwell in the midst of a people of unclean lips; for my eyes have seen the King, the LORD of hosts!"*

Ezekiel fell on his face.

Ezekiel 1:28 *As the appearance of the rainbow in the clouds on a rainy day, so was the appearance of the surrounding radiance. Such was the appearance of the likeness of the glory of the LORD. And when I saw it, I fell on my face and heard a voice speaking.*

The disciples fell on their faces.

Matthew 17:5 *He was still speaking when, behold, a bright cloud overshadowed them, and a voice from the cloud said, "This is my beloved Son, with whom I am well pleased; listen to him." When the disciples heard this, they fell on their faces and were terrified. But Jesus came and touched them, saying, "Rise, and have no fear."*

John fell as though dead.

Revelation 1:17 *When I saw him, I fell at his feet as though dead. But he laid his right hand on me, saying, "Fear not, I am the first and the last, and the living one. I died, and behold I am alive forevermore, and I have the keys of Death and Hades.*

Simon Peter fell down, confessed his sin and said, "Depart from me."

Luke 5:3 *Getting into one of the boats, which was Simon's, he asked him to put out a little from the land. And he sat down and taught the people from the boat. And when he had finished speaking, he said to Simon, "Put out into the deep and let down your nets for a catch." And Simon answered, "Master, we toiled all night and took nothing! But at your word I will let down the nets." And when they had done this, they enclosed a large number of fish, and their nets were breaking. They signaled to their partners in the other boat to come and help them. And they came and filled both the boats, so that they began to sink. But when Simon Peter saw it, he fell down at Jesus' knees, saying, "Depart from me, for I am a sinful man, O Lord."*

Faultless, Standing Before God

FAULTLESS

God is praised because He is able to make us stand before Himself as He really is, in all His glory. We will stand there faultless and full of joy. When He says we'll stand before Him faultless, He doesn't just mean positionally, but that God has removed all our sins from us. The new nature will have met together with a transformed body in which there is no longer the presence of the sinful flesh nature. We will be without blemish before Him and fully righteous, able to stand before Him without fear or shrinking away.

GREAT JOY - EXUBERANT JOY

Instead, we will be transformed and able to stand in heaven before our Maker, full of joy. Not only will we have joy, but there will be a divine joy in heaven over us, over the fellowship of His redeemed people. In fact, we're taught that even now when there's a sinner saved, there's joy in heaven. God will rejoice over what He has done in us for the glory of His own name.

Luke 15:7 *Just so, I tell you, there will be more joy in heaven over one sinner who repents than over ninety-nine righteous persons who need no repentance.*

Zephaniah 3:17 *"The LORD your God is in your midst, A victorious warrior. He will exult over you with joy, He will be quiet in His love, He will rejoice over you with shouts of joy.* (NASB)

The One Who is alone (the only God)

We should always remember the uniqueness of God. The one, true, living God is worthy of our praise. He is the **only** God who exists, and the **only** one capable of bringing these things to pass. There will be no boasting in heaven. God has saved sinners in such a way that there is no room for boasting on our part.

The One Who is accessible (through Christ)

Though He is unique, though He alone is God, He is not apart from us in such a way that He is not able to be known. He didn't have to make Himself known, but it was right that He would demonstrate Who He is and demonstrate His glory. He enables us to fellowship with Him, enjoy Him, love Him, and serve Him. He can be both be our teacher and our Father. All this is possible because God saved us through Jesus Christ our Lord. Our praise will flow to God through Jesus Christ. All these blessings have come to us through Him.

Contrary to what most American evangelicals seem to believe, Jesus is the **only** way to God, the **only** way to heaven, and the **only** way to eternal life. It is **only** through Christ that God is accessible. Apart from Christ, God cannot be known. Apart from Christ, God cannot be worshipped or followed. It is through Christ that God has been made known. This is how His blessings have come to us and this is how our praises are acceptable to Him.

THE ONES OFFERING THIS PRAISE

The ones to be kept (from stumbling)

If you look at the road to Heaven from a human point of view, you see lots of land mines present, things that could ruin a person's faith. You then see your own lack of inherent ability to go through that jungle successfully, and you realize that He is guarding you and keeping you in the faith. You will have a heart full of thankfulness, offering praise for His grace.

The ones to be presented (faultless)

One day we will stand before God in His glory without the fear and dread that we'd have if we were still sinful. We will be forgiven, not just positionally righteous, but truly righteous, because of what He has done for us. As a result, there will be great rejoicing. We will be unshackled from all of that which now grieves us, from all that now hinders our fervency, from all that now hinders everything we want to be in Christ.

The ones who know God

We offer praise because we can know and **do** know the **one and only true God.** We've been delivered from lies and from false gods; delivered to the true God. Though we don't deserve it, we know God as Savior and Jesus as Lord.

THE PRAISE THAT IS OFFERED—TO HIM BE:

Glory—The glory of God is the sum total of all His attributes. *To Him...be glory*—God's nature and character. We don't praise God when we water down the truth about who He is.

Majesty—He is King, a great King who rules over what He has created. God is to be loved, honored and submitted to. He is majestic.

Dominion—GOD is over all, everything and everyone. He rules over all peoples, heaven, hell, the earth, the universe—ALL, every single day.

Authority—What God commands ALWAYS gets accomplished. Some imagine they can resist His will, but then discover they can't. God has been God FOREVER. There never has been a moment without Him, and there never will be. He is the same today as He always has been and will be.

Jude ends this letter with *Amen*—so be it. This is true!

SELF-TEST

Before we finish, whether or not you're using the study questions at the back, think through the questions on this page. It would be tragic to have studied Jude without applying it.

1. Am I in the faith? Do I have saving faith in Christ?
2. Do I see the dangers to my faith? Do I see that they are real and powerful and that apart from God I would surely fall away?
3. Do I realize why I don't fall away, and won't fall away? Is my heart grateful that God is keeping me by His own power?
4. Do I concentrate on my future? Do I think about standing before God, faultless and in great joy? Does that fill my heart with praise right now? Do I read this, and say with Jude at the end, Amen?

Study Questions – 2 and 3 John and Jude

Chapter 1—Truth and Love—2 John 1-3

1. Why is truth important?
2. What can we learn from the fact that John referred to himself as *the elder?*
3. What connection is there between age and spiritual maturity? (Can you think of some examples of spiritually maturity among the people you know?)
4. Can you explain the two theories as to who *the elect lady and her children* are? What difference, if any, will it make in your interpretation of the rest of 2 John?
5. How does the word *elect* speak of God's sovereignty in salvation? What do we mean when we say He is sovereign?
6. Do you think often of God's choice of you, and thank Him for it?
7. Why are truth and love not enemies?
8. Why would John and *all who know the truth* love the elect lady and her children?
9. Is there a difference between grace and mercy?
10. How do grace and mercy relate to peace?
11. Does the truth abide (that is, take up residence) within you? How can that be? What does it mean to you personally?

Chapter 2—The Joy of Godly People—2 John 4-6

1. What did the aged apostle rejoice in?
2. "Whatever brings joy to our hearts is a commentary on our spiritual condition, our spiritual concerns and our spiritual maturity." Do you agree? What are your greatest joys these days?
3. Have you seen churches or ministries that promote only part of the truth of the gospel, not all of the truth? What are some parts of the truth about Jesus that are often neglected?
4. Look over the bulleted list of things to rejoice over. Can your church's leaders rejoice to see you doing those things?
5. What is John's commandment? When is it easy for you to obey it? When is it hard? Will you obey it today?

6. When was the last time someone exhorted you to <u>live</u> the love of God, to walk in it? When was the last time you urged someone else to do it?
7. How does your obedience to God connect to your love for God and your love for God's people?
8. How can truth without love be harmful?
9. What's wrong with just having truth without love?
10. Can you think of any concrete ways that you can help other believers to set their joy on the things that are eternal—on Jesus and on the things that are true?

Chapter 3—Truth, Love and Deceivers—2 John 7-11

1. Before this study, have you spent much time thinking about the possibility of deceivers in the church? Why or why not?
2. How are false teaching and immoral behavior connected?
3. Who or what is the ultimate source of false teaching?
4. What do truth and love do for the community (for the church), as explained here?
5. Can you think of examples of entire churches or denominations that have abandoned truth, abandoned love, or both? If so, how would that abandonment have started? (Caution: Truth is what God says, not what you think about what God says, nor what you wish God had said. Godly love is love that comes from God, love that includes love for those who are walking in truth.)
6. How will a commitment to both truth and love defend or protect the community?
7. "False teachers are known not only by what they say, but by what they refuse to acknowledge and what they will not say." What are some parts of the truth which some teachers today won't acknowledge?
8. What is wrong with each of these statements?
    a. Jesus and the Father are the same person. (This is the belief of "Oneness Pentecostals.")
    b. God the Father became a man.
    c. Jesus is a god, but not the mighty God. (This is the belief of the Jehovah's Witnesses.)
    d. Jesus was a good teacher and a prophet, but nothing more.
    e. Jesus is the literal spirit-brother of Lucifer, a created being. (This has been taught by Latter-Day Saints.)

9. How can exposing false teachers be an act of love?
10. What's the difference between confronting false teaching as an act of love, and confronting false teaching as an act of pride? How can we maintain love while standing vigorously for the truth?

Chapter 4—Truth, Love and Drawing the Lines—2 John 7-11

1. Explain the difference between starting in the truth and continuing in the truth. Have you been entertaining teaching that doesn't accord with the truth?
2. What specific dangers do the false teachers bring into the church?
3. Why, in your opinion, are church leaders and individual Christians often so reluctant to deal with false teachers?
4. Have you been assisting someone who is leading others astray?
5. If a person whom you love, a person in your church, starts teaching falsehood, what will you do?
   a. How will you deal with that in love?
   b. How will you watch yourself, in order to protect yourself and God's flock?
   c. How will you deal with both the possibility that the person merely doesn't know better, and the possibility that the person is a false teacher who is a huge danger?
6. If the false teachers are not opposed, what sort of reward could be lost? By whom?
7. Are you more concerned with how men view you than how God views you? Or maybe more concerned with academic respectability than with Biblical fidelity?
8. Is it possible for someone who is truly converted to depart from the teachings of Christ and to stay gone?

Chapter 5—True Fellowship—2 John 12-13

1. What's the main problem with efforts to reproduce New Testament Christianity and its culture?
2. "The church is counter-cultural, because it is to be like Heaven, not like the world." In what ways is your church like Heaven? Suppose you were asked to help plan a large meeting for your church. What are some worldly things that you've heard of churches doing, that you would want to avoid?
3. Where does Christian fellowship come from?

4. Are you in the fellowship? Do you know Jesus as Lord and Savior? Do you know the fellowship that is with the Father and with the Son, and therefore, with every true child of God? Do you know the supernatural reality that you didn't know before you were saved?
5. What are some things you could do to help maintain the fellowship?
6. What are some evidences of true Christian fellowship?
7. What would be evidences of a lack of true Christian fellowship? That is, how is Christian fellowship different from the fellowship you could have with unbelievers at a business event or at a civic organization?
8. Think of your church while reading through the bullet points in the section marked "True Fellowship is Principled." Are there one or two areas where you could strengthen your church's fellowship?
9. Do you enjoy being with your Christian brothers and sisters?
10. Is your view of Christian fellowship founded in salvation and submissive to God and to God's word?

Chapter 6—People of the Truth—3 John 1-8

1. How do the following statements agree or disagree with the idea of the existence of truth?
    a. "That may be true for you, but I see it differently."
    b. "It's intolerant to say that your religious beliefs are right and everyone else is wrong.
    c. "All roads lead to heaven."
    d. "I'm sure that I don't know everything, but there are some things that I'm sure of."
    e. "Truth is always evolving."
    f. "Just follow your heart."
2. Which would be more likely to be useful—a theology book from 1750 or a science textbook from 1950? Why?
3. In what sense or senses is the church formed by the truth?
4. In what sense or senses is the church formed for the truth?
5. How does a knowledge of truth and the love of truth impact how you express love to other people?
6. As you read through 3 John, does John strike you as cold-hearted, or full of love, or in between? What about the Lord Jesus, who said, "I am…the truth"—Was He emotionally cold? What about

you—are you able to combine fixed truth with deep love for people?

7. Have you ever rejoiced to hear that someone else was walking in the truth?

8. Gaius had been hospitable. Why was the nature of his guests important?

9. In what four ways did John characterize Gaius's hospitality?

10. How can you or your church be more like Gaius? How can you be more like the apostle John?

Chapter 7—Truth Models—3 John 9-15

1. What's the difference between Gaius and Diotrephes? What might a "Diotrephes" look like in the church today?

2. Why are we unable to simply "restore the New Testament church"? Is restoring the New Testament church a good goal?

3. Why does every church have problems?

4. Can you think of any biblical principles that will help a church know how to deal with problems?

5. "No one should ever be in a position of spiritual authority who hasn't demonstrated and isn't committed to submission to authority." Is this a new thought for you?

6. What's behind Diotrephes's rebellion?

7. What specific things has he done wrong?

8. Switching from Diotrephes to Demetrius, in what way or ways is Demetrius a good example?

9. Who have you imitated in the past? Are there people who have been heroes for you—people who have been models for you? If so, were they godly people?

10. While remembering that nobody but Jesus is perfect in every way, list a few people who are good models for you. For each one of them, list in what way or ways that person is a good, godly model.

11. Who is imitating you? If they walk on the pathway you're on, is it safe? Is it spiritually healthy?

12. How can you be a better model?

Chapter 8 – Called, Loved and Kept – Jude 1-2

1. Why are you studying Jude? Is there anything you hope to get from this study?

2. Why is Jude often neglected?

3. What do we know about the author? What's unusual about him, compared to other New Testament authors?
4. Can you explain the two kinds of calling in the New Testament?
5. What does God's love have to do with our calling?
6. In what sense are believers kept? Does that make a difference in how you live your life? If so, in what way?
7. What three things does Jude want to be multiplied for his readers? Is there one that's more meaningful for you today than the others? Is there one that is an area in which you sense a need to grow more?
8. The author says, "We can have confidence about believers in times of turmoil." Do you need to apply that to your thinking about some believers you know? Do you need to apply it to yourself?
9. Do you see any serious dangers facing today's church? If so, what sort of dangers?
10. Are you, or believers around you, in the midst of turmoil? If so, is there a sense of calm despite the turmoil? What will happen if you and others pray for mercy, peace and love be multiplied to you and to those believers you know who are in turmoil?

Chapter 9 – Change of Plans – Jude 3-4

1. Have you ever felt compelled by God to change a plan, even though the plan had seemed godly?
2. Jude was urging his readers to contend earnestly for the faith. What attitudes would the words "contend earnestly for" usually bring to mind? What is the first thing the author mentions that should mark our attitude as we contend for the faith?
3. Why is it necessary to contend for the faith? What can happen to the truth if we don't contend for it?
4. How can God's power encourage you as you contend for the faith?
5. Who must contend for the faith?
6. What things can we know about dangerous people in the church? Without gossiping, can you think of instances when you've seen or heard of spiritually dangerous people in the church?
7. What things mark the character of these dangerous people?
8. What can we say about their actions?
9. What can we say about their teachings?
10. Are you willing to admit that such dangers exist, and to deal with them in a godly way? What steps have you taken in that direction?

Chapter 10 – This Condemnation – Jude 5-7

1. What is apostasy?
2. Have you ever heard a sermon on the TV or radio about the dangers of apostasy? If not, what might be the reasons?
3. What other books of the Bible warn us about apostasy? Are they all from the same human author?
4. What three pictures from the past does Jude use to remind us of the judgment that is coming for those who defect from the truth?
5. Did the Israelites in the wilderness think they were failing to believe the Lord? That is, did they think they were abandoning Him? What happened to them?
6. What is the author's interpretation of the angels mentioned in Jude 6?
7. What two sins of those angels does Jude mention? What consequences did those angels face? (Are they now past those consequences?)
8. What were the sins of Sodom and Gomorrah? What was the result for them?
9. What does Psalm 73 tell us about how to guard ourselves against moving away from the Lord?
10. Are you guarding against slippage from the faith in your own life? Are you helping others do that?

Chapter 11 – Serious Danger – Jude 8-11

1. The author says, "We live in a day of unholy tolerance—tolerating sin and error, but not tolerating truth." Do you see examples of that?
2. In what sense is it madness to be bold in opposing the Lord and His truth?
3. In what ways are the people Jude is describing bold?
4. "Mature saints are the most mindful of matters of authority." Why would this be the case?
5. What were these unholy, bold people relying on?
6. What two kinds of apostates does this chapter mention? Can you explain the difference between them?
7. In what ways are these people (who may be intelligent and very highly educated) ignorant?
8. What sort of ambition do these people have?
9. How are they like Cain?

10. How are they like Balaam?
11. How are they like Korah?
12. How can you apply the warnings of Jude?

Chapter 12 – Serious Danger, part 2 – Unholy Presence – Jude 12-13

1. These unholy people are like what five things in nature?
2. Which of those five resonates more with you? Why?
3. What do hidden reefs, waterless clouds and fruitless autumn trees have in common?
4. What are some of the influences these people have in the church?
5. This should be a scary thought, but do you see any of these marks in your own life?
6. "For true shepherds, the church is not a job. It's a calling." What might be some signs that a church leader is focused on his own power or prestige or profit instead of on feeding the flock? How can we protect the church from such people while also not making false accusations against a leader we don't like or don't understand?
7. What is the ultimate destiny of these false teachers?
8. If others look to you for godly wisdom, have you taught them of the danger of false teachers? Have you taught them how to recognize them?
9. Are you willing to stand against those who are false? Are you willing to do it with a motivation of love for the Lord and for His church, not a "gotcha" motivation of finding things and people to condemn?

Chapter 13 – Their Judgment Foretold – Jude 14-16

1. The author says, "This is not a parable, myth or legend, but a future reality that is being described so that we would be warned." What happens when we turn Scripture reality into myth or legend?
2. What do you know about Enoch? For more information, see Genesis 5:18-24 and Hebrews 11:5. Enoch was also an ancestor of Noah thus of Jesus (Luke 3:37) and of everyone else now living on earth.
3. Abraham lived about 4000 years ago. Enoch lived before that. He prophesied about such people. Do prophecies have a "use by" date when they expire?
4. Who will judge these dangerous people?
5. What will make the judgment dramatic?

6. In what way is false teaching "against him"—that is, against the Lord?
7. These people are in the church. They may be very religious. What is ungodly about them?
8. In verse 16, what five things does Jude tell us about these people's character?
9. Are you tempted to display one or more of these bad character traits in the church?
10. "Those who don't know Jesus ... need to know that He is willing to forgive, on His terms." How does that statement relate to the danger that these verses warn us about?

Chapter 14 – The Believer's Response to Apostasy – Jude 17-23

1. Before reading this book, were you familiar with the word apostate? What is an apostate?
2. Have apostates become clearly evident in any churches that you know of?
3. Will the church become better and better, so that in the last days before Jesus comes, there are almost no false Christians?
4. Why would apostates be divisive? (Do you think that they are likely to admit that they are the ones causing the divisions?)
5. How will our reaction to apostates and false teachers be different if we know that they are worldly and without the Holy Spirit?
6. When dealing with apostasy, why is it important to keep ourselves in the love of God?
7. Jude says we're to be "building yourselves up in your most holy faith." What's that mean? How do we do that?
8. Are you more tempted to be over-harsh on straying people, without trying to rescue them, or are you more tempted to accept both them and their sin? How can these verses speak to your temptation?
9. How often do you think about the Lord's return? How does thinking about his return motivate us concerning our dealings with error in the church?

Chapter 15 – Doxology – Jude 24-25

1. Consider the four questions at the end of this chapter.
2. What wonderful truths about God can you see mentioned or referenced in these two verses? (Can you find at least four? Six? Or more?)
3. What does it mean when Jude speaks of the One who is able to keep you from stumbling?
4. What happens when ordinary people see some of God's glory? What would explain this?
5. How will true Christians be different when seeing Jesus from how they are now?
6. Why will there be joy in that day? Can you think of more than one reason?
7. What or who can keep us safe despite all of the evil work of false teachers and other temptations in this life?

ABOUT THE AUTHOR

Richard Caldwell Jr. is the senior pastor at Founders Baptist Church in Spring, Texas. He is married to Jacquelyn, and they have four children and three grandchildren. He has served in pastoral ministry for 33 years, in the roles of youth pastor, church planter, and senior pastor. He is a graduate of Southwestern Baptist Theological Seminary (M.Div.) and The Master's Seminary (D.Min). He is one of seven campus pastors for The Expositor's Seminary, and also serves as a faculty member. Richard's sermons can be heard weekdays on radio (Walking in Grace) in the city of Houston, and on Sermon Audio (http://www.sermonaudio.com).

www.ingramcontent.com/pod-product-compliance
Lightning Source LLC
Chambersburg PA
CBHW072025040426
42447CB00009B/1737